Crossing the Rift:
North Carolina Poets on 9/11 & Its Aftermath

# CROSSING THE RIFT

*North Carolina Poets on 9/11 & Its Aftermath*

Edited by
Joseph Bathanti
David Potorti

Press 53
Winston-Salem

Press 53, LLC
PO Box 30314
Winston-Salem, NC 27130

First Edition

Cover image of twenty-five-year-old French aerialist Philippe Petit making his unauthorized tightrope walk between the newly built twin towers of the World Trade Center in New York City on August 7, 1974: AP Photo / Alan Welner

Cover Design by Claire V. Foxx and Kevin Morgan Watson

Interior Design and Layout by Kevin Morgan Watson

Library of Congress Control Number
2021943444

ISBN 978-1-950413-37-9 (softcover)
ISBN 978-1-950413-38-6 (hardcover)

Dedication

*To those who died on September 11
and those who continue to die as an outcome of September 11*

# Contents

# Preface

The inspiration for *Crossing the Rift: North Carolina Poets on 9/11 & Its Aftermath* actually began, all the way back in September of 2010, just prior to the ninth anniversary of 9/11. David Potorti, then the Arts Tourism Manager at the North Carolina Arts Council (NCAC), mused with me offhandedly over assembling a complement of poems to memorialize the tenth anniversary of 9/11. By June of 2011, we had laid concrete plans, and David, now Literature Director at NCAC, and I enlisted the assistance of Cathy Smith Bowers, then serving as North Carolina's Poet Laureate.

In August of 2011, we sent out the call: "to commemorate and acknowledge in poetry the upcoming 10th anniversary of 9/11 . . . a poem that in some way [touched] directly on the events of 9/11 or [reflected] associated themes of peace, hope, reconciliation, loss, etc." The poems harvested were posted, in the order they arrived, each day leading up to 9/11, on the Poet Laureate section of NCAC's blog.

As the twentieth anniversary of 9/11 loomed, David and I agreed to edit a print anthology, much larger in scope and ambition than its digital predecessor, and involving many more poets and voices from all across North Carolina. While we remained preoccupied with our original themes, we were also very aware that the lenses and sensibilities through which to view and write about 9/11 had grown exponentially. Tuesday, September 11, 2001, is a day that has, in so many ways, dramatically set the agenda for the twenty-first century: Islamophobia, the vilification of immigrants and the undocumented, ramped-up xenophobia, nationalism, and isolationism. It unleashed war and supercharged military budgets that continue to impoverish our nation, with accompanying losses of community, health, and hope, and concurrent rises in homophobia, transphobia, virulent racism, and domestic terrorism.

The wounds of 9/11 are many: physical, environmental, and psychic. The war in Afghanistan, begun in response to the attacks in 2001, is now twenty years old. The war in Iraq, begun in 2003, has metastasized into regional conflicts that terrorize local populations and set tens of thousands of refugees in motion. We've witnessed our weapons of war return to our own streets where they are turned on peaceful protests. We separate children from their parents at the border. The very form of government we celebrate and sought to preserve after 9/11 is under assault from within. It feels as if we've lived, for the past two decades, in a liminal space.

What's more, David and I realized that an entire generation of poets—infants and children when 9/11 occurred, and even those yet to be born—has been irrevocably influenced by the legacy of that day. We wondered, in our call to the poets of *Crossing the Rift*, how the specter and legacy of 9/11 had infiltrated and influenced their consciousness and perceptions, their central preoccupations as poets.

What follows in these pages takes into account, from myriad unforgettable perspectives, the impact of the vast collateral fallout associated with 9/11, how that day led us, as poets, to this juncture. These poems give moving and palpable testimony to what Carolyn Forche calls "the poetry of witness"—a ritual act of reconciliation through language; a renewed sense of shared humanity and righteous resistance; and, perhaps most importantly, a sacred vow to never forget.

The great Samuel Beckett reminds us that "Words are all we have." The aspiration of this volume is to brave the rift, the breach, that only words can begin, however precariously, to mend. *Crossing the Rift* is not merely an overture of goodwill and ongoing vigilance, but of will itself—embodied in the very words of the intrepid poets in this anthology.

Joseph Bathanti

# Introduction

My brother Jim died in the September 11 attacks.

Fifteen years earlier, he and the World Trade Center appeared in one of my favorite family photos. My father is in the foreground, not much older than I am today, and strolling a short distance behind are my mother and Jim. The Brooklyn Heights Promenade where they're walking overlooks the East River, and, beyond, Manhattan, where the twin towers rise in the background. It was a balmy Thanksgiving, when we'd cooked turkey and sweet potatoes and drank Beaujolais Nouveau.

It was jarring to look at that photo after 9/11 and consider how the events of that day cleaved in two not only my family, but also the world in which we lived. The seamless passage of time across holidays and gatherings split into a before and after, a then and now, a sense of certainty and expectation overshadowed by unpredictability and a kind of betrayal. Hadn't we been safe? Hadn't airport traffic been the hardest part of flying? Hadn't the festival of faces, and nationalities, and neighborhoods been the best part of living in New York? Could memory be trusted?

Love and support poured out from all quarters after the attacks: casseroles and cards from neighbors in North Carolina, where I now lived, phone calls and emails from high school and college friends, Mass cards and prayers. But it went far beyond that—Americans across the country mobilized to help, classrooms of kids collected money, Texans hitched up barbecue smokers and drove cross country to cook for the 9/11 relief crews. I heard about candlelight vigils in Iran, Russians sobbing in the streets, Muslims praying. These natural expressions of human solidarity reflected my mother's words at the time of my brother's death: "I don't want anyone else to have to feel the pain I'm feeling right now."

It was a shared sentiment at first, and as I sought an alternative to the cold reality of what had occurred, I found relief in the voices of poets, artists and writers. Their words gave me the balm of metaphor, the right-sizing of historical context, a way of dealing with feelings that were too big for me to handle.

But people's instinct for compassion quickly channeled elsewhere, into hatred of the other, an excuse for new military escapades, and a hardening of attitudes, suspicions and beliefs about their fellow citizens.

However, the event also unleashed a cascade of reflections and ruminations that run counter to these responses. I'm heartened to find that many of the most vibrant, diverse voices expanding the dialogue and the lenses through which we see 9/11 and its aftermath come from members of my own community of poets in North Carolina. Their observations and exhortations, and their simple witness, ground us in humanity, link us in concern for one another, and forge paths far beyond violence and war. Their words illuminate our shared wounds and our shared grief across time and place. They suggest that September 11, 2001 was not the first day that parents wept, children were traumatized, and families torn apart, nor was it the last. And they tell us there is much work to be done: to expand our compassion, to grieve genuinely and deeply, and to make common cause with each other, with our environment, and with the larger world.

Most of all, I hope their words make it safe to remember: to remember my brother and all those who perished; to remember who we were, and aspire to be; and to remember the world that we lived in, not through some sentimental filter, but with a renewed sense of our connectedness and shared future. I'm grateful for their words.

David Potorti

# CROSSING
# THE RIFT

*North Carolina Poets on 9/11 & Its Aftermath*

## Ars Memorativa

> *Simonides was enabled by his recollection of the place in which each of [the banqueters] had been reclining at table to identify them for separate interment; and that this circumstance suggested to him the discovery of the truth that the best aid to clearness of memory consists in orderly arrangement.* —Cicero's *De Oratore II* [353]

In Manhattan we might catch a glimpse
of Simonides on West Street pushing
a grocery cart, looking for the twin youths.

Once they summoned him to the entrance
of the banquet hall before it collapsed
on host and banqueters seated at table.

At Ground Zero, he searches for some sign
of Castor and Pollux in their gleaming robes
of aluminum, stainless steel and glass.

What harrowed panegyric can he chant
when the bruised mind is purpled
by the caved-in memory?

His song is flattened space, the lyrics smashed,
the heinous imagery squeezed,
compressed and buried in broken lines.

If mnemonics could recreate the Towers
in the mind like two Interior Castles,
we could sweep each office cubicle's hearth,
to identify the ashen faces.

Since the incinerated relics vanished,
memory would then surrender the names
of the dead to beaming vaults of light.

Sheer skyscrapers rise from terror's abyss
to constellate with Gemini's twin stars.

## This Innocent Sky

On a beautiful summer morning, sky clear,
Phillipe Petit steps into the air between the towers.
*On a beautiful autumn morning, sky clear,*
*bodies hurtle through the air between the towers.*

Philippe Petit steps into the air between the towers
he tests his line as if stepping into an icy pond—
*bodies hurtle through the air between the towers*
*strewn by the monstrous force that drove the planes.*

He tests his line as if stepping into an icy pond
he walks to the center and gazes at the streets below
*Strewn by the monstrous force that drove the planes*
*survivors cling to the narrow windows with gasping breaths.*

He walks to the center and gazes at the streets below
then lies down on his line and watches passing gulls.
*Survivors cling to the narrow windows with gasping breaths.*
*Cell phones carry burning words of love.*

He lies down on his line and watches passing gulls,
police on either side attempt to call him home.
*Cell phones carry burning words of love*
*Sirens scream from Brooklyn and beyond.*

Police on either side attempt to call him home.
He smiles at them, happier than he has ever been.
*Sirens scream from Brooklyn and beyond*
*Masses huddle on the streets, their mouths agape.*

He smiles at them, happier than he has ever been,
he floats beyond time, here in this innocent sky.
*Masses huddle on the streets, their mouths agape*
*as the flames pour out, the buildings start to shake.*

He floats beyond time, here in this innocent sky,
floats for thirty-seven years, his dream preserved
*until the flames pour out, the buildings start to shake*
*the floors implode, dissolve into a cloud of noxious dust.*

He floats for thirty-seven years, his dream preserved
until, on this autumn morning, sky so clear
*the floors implode, dissolve into a cloud of noxious dust*
*where Philippe Petit, on a summer morning, once stepped into the air.*

# You of the Long Shadow

Now on Route 124
closing the distance between
my gritty exit on the Garden State Parkway and the much prettier one
that takes me to the university where I study and teach,
my husband calls me on the small black cell phone
we keep in the car for emergencies.

He tells me about the Twin Towers.
I walk dazed into the student lounge.
All the televisions are on. We watch together
as the towers fall.
No, not fall.
They deflate, like a souffle taken too soon out of the oven.
They fold inward,
neatly,
save for the sugary powder that plumes, that
(like that other plume in '45)
crawled into the still breathing lungs, slowly killing them for years to come.

On that day, we knew none of that.
We saw—without understanding the extent of what is to come—
two straight buildings crumble into their own long shadows.

In the class I teach on World Literature—

and which I did not cancel because the gravity of what we saw did not hit
    us yet, and because, in truth,
I had been a student in a part of the world where atrocities are for every
    day class attendance,
where buildings exploded,
did not fold inward neatly,
the bedrooms, the dining tables, the tea set on top, lay bare, gaping out of
wall-less apartments, the rebar piercing the sky, the curtains billowing out
into the windowless air

—a student whose mother works at the Pentagon and had narrowly avoided the fate of the people folded into the tower's shadow when the plane destined for her plunged elsewhere, looked at me in a way I still refuse to see in my mind's eye.
I mention it here. But I refuse to see it again.
After class, my advisor tells me it's best if I go home.
I must have forgotten that I was Arab and Muslim.

But she remembered.

At home, I watched an interview with a Jordanian woman my mother knew crying for her son who worked in one of the towers. She cried the way Arab women cry over their martyred sons, full throatedly.

It is a platitude to say that everything changed after that, but it is true. To others, I became a different person. They asked me different questions, so I pursued different answers.

The towers' long shadows overtook us. We folded neatly into them.

## Sunbathing and News of War

Spring break, 2003

I lie belly flat on a straw mat,
Emerald Isle so many worlds away from war.

I press with my palms just here and there
to make a gully for my cheek,
settling in perhaps to nap,
to forget the mound of unread essays I left at home.
Left at home because I swear to you
I am not thinking of them.

Stiff Atlantic breezes
style and restyle my hair,
sun begins to redden the rims of my ears.
My mind is wholly on creature comforts—
sand, sun, wind on wintered skin.

And I swear I do not imagine
wounded in Iraqi hospitals
lining looted hallways hoping
for amputations,
the arms of their dutiful family
raised hour after hour,
holding life-sustaining drips.
          Such gravity.

I swear I do not wonder what those aching
heaven-raised arms must feel
after such a time in such unnatural position—
between survivor's guilt and grief
how much hope remains, how much hope
does it take to hold them up?

I raise myself on my own weak arms
and try to hold my own chin up
long enough to feel
the unnatural bend
break into ache,
long enough to tremble
at this merely awkward stupid suffering
while worlds way—
you know what is happening
worlds away. . . .

# Asides

September 11, 2001

On a sun-drenched street, one man looked up just in time
to see hundreds of pigeons startle skyward just
before unbearable impact. Their reflection
shaped a flag of shadow on glass buildings
split-seconds before the image flew into shards,
a confetti of knives, and the birds
gone into a suddenly darkening sky.

It's said a woman in a Brooklyn kitchen turned
to see clouds in her window-glass, a backyard
filling with white paper, drifts of it shining
in sunlight but edged with the ink-black
of old-fashioned death letters. Beneath a sky
grown smoky with erasure, she turned toward
the new weather, alien snow bearing
the incomprehensible signatures of fire.

A man looked out an office window toward
other offices like his on another street,
felt close thunder first, and then—
for one tick of the clock—heard a huge
music he took to be beautiful, took to be
an inexplicable waterfall, gravity and silver
rivers at their play. Until he shivered
into seeing falling glass, the new Deluge.

All over Europe, and in Vietnam, in Russia,
China, Greece, Cambodia, Rwanda, Tibet—
were there answering shadows, a dimming
of lights?
            Imperceptible ash, might the dead
of a century's wars have risen
like motes for a moment?

                    In the Hiroshima Museum
a sunshaft continued to bend, flowering again
and again within a vase of melted glass.
In countries made of blood-feud and sand,
didn't women turn from murmured prayers
toward the sky's answer, blank blue
point-blank burning glass?

And here, as in the slant light of every September,
caterpillars moved slowly along the turning leaves;
the cricket opened and shut his rusted door
into autumn; one particular firefly went out,
last low star of the season, indifferent
as a nova to what men have made.
                              Our marvelous
looking-glass holds, in its network of steel
and invisible signal, history and myth
and money laid across the world.
That great snare shines in its cables
like the orb-weaver's art, trembles fragile
as any web on night grass
                    in a field of starlight.

# Hoping for More

for Sherry and Joe


Mid 2003,
baby cousin gets called into the second gulf war almost by accident,
deciding to be all the man he could be after floundering
for years past high school. he signs up
for the marines of all things. the day
he is to report, there he is calling the shots.
he has his mom baking cookies and other things
to remind him of home.
as he packs his duffle bag,
a knock at the door, and they swoop in.
two men, in their pressed uniforms, announce:
"you won't need those where you're going."
"we always pick up our own," they tell his stunned mom.
they go, bag full of hope
and desire. his manhood on the line,
he ships off to bootcamp before landing in kuwait
for a stint. he is in the desert, fixing tanks
that bog down in sand, no machine made
to best the shifting dunes. so, after an inquiry
about his wellbeing, i learn about the need for care packages,
and we send: assorted cookies, candy bars, cologne and baby wipes.
the desert has no toilet paper for the men,
we are told. dust fills every crack,
so wipes it is for the troops. the boxes flow.
every month his mom sends one, and on the following month,
i send the next. in between,
we send prayers.

# Because a Doorway

for Tony, 82nd Airborne, Iraqi Freedom 2003

can be an ambush
when you're in the shop,

the gritting sound
of the metal grinder

flinting fire into the air,
or the arc of light

flashing blue
hot above the weld pool

to form a joint, I stand
outside the open doorway,

calling your name,
waiting for you to turn

and lift the dark shield
of your welding helmet

to see me—
known, and unarmed

I wait
to see your shoulders

soften before I cross
the threshold.

# The Wakeful Bird Sings Darkling

Our tiny plot of a cottage was cloaked
in pine at the graveled close of a sidestreet,
undercover, overgrown, September sprawl
of raspberries lost again to the blackbirds.
The sun could never find its way
to our windows; the walls were thick
as a bunker's, stolid, stone and stone
and stone. The baby sick again,
as he was for most of his first year,
his fevered sleep fast in my arms. That morning
the phone rang, my husband out in his real life,
calling just from work, but the line staticked
and broken as if from a great distance,
saying to turn on the TV. And so I did,
just in time to see the first tower fall, then
the slant silent drift of a plane, the little bloom
of fire, the smoke's ashen pillar and pall.
The baby's glittering eyes fixed only on me.

We went out back then, sat on the crumbling stoop,
where just three months before our yellow cat,
Rover, had dragged himself after a stroke.
Back left paw trailing, curled under, his pupils
faint pinpricks of terror. *Lamb of God,*
my husband would call it when he draped him,
purring, like a stole over his shoulders,
but on his last day he wouldn't even let me touch him,
hissing from the closet's dark. The vet
had to come for him, wearing falconer's gloves.

That September morning's iris of sky just as fierce,
stripped and raw, too close; I shielded the baby
with my shadow. Then the quiet was ripped
by the ratchet of a kingfisher plummeting
from the power lines into the dark mirror
of our pond. The world a dim window
I couldn't see through, my focus only this
instant, this infant listless and flushed
in my arms. I whispered the rapid count
of his breaths per minute, trying
to determine the line between self-reliance
and when we'd need help.

## Home Security after 9/11

*Consent: if the police show up at your door and ask you if they can come inside to search and you consent to the search, then the police do not need a warrant.*

At the break of moon, a front door Herculesed
to pine dust, children dreaming of [      ].
Forced from sleep,

dogs shepherd us into a nightened cave
where a mother is crying, *Let me grab a scarf, just a scarf.*
Bleary brained in its meteor glow, static shouts belling
the block, I believe

we are being abducted by [      ].
I ask the low white light, Where will all the Muslims go?
Blue men bustle me into their van, everything a slow
lucent swing, lashed stiff in this effigy. An old blister

bursts. Blood sieges
the street in a crucible of war.
It pummels the god-prince. It pleads for [      ].

*Plain view: police do not need a search warrant to seize evidence that is in plain view of a place where the police are legally authorized to be.*

Hours later, escorted inside for some Reese's Puffs
before school, "Number One Dad" mug
in a behemoth's hands.

A maggot nibbles through my nostril
as I munch, the violent violation. "Red Nation" rises
from a radio, Lil Wayne plopping *Tough luck* into my
breakfast bowl. *Pour me*

*another cup you filthy [　　],*
the behemoth snarls through the cage of his teeth.
I do it when he shifts, shows his [　　], shiny as
a scourge of blood, says, *This right here*

*is your Allah.*
        How many moments like these
seared into my timeline, unchangeable as 9/11?
I am aware
        of many things: the softening cereal,
my paper-thin lungs. That there is no boundary
of [　　] in a body.

*Is the person whose home or property being investigated/searched
expected a degree of privacy? Was that expectation objectively
reasonable? i.e., would society as a whole agree that the place or
thing should remain private?*

        It would seem the exits want to keep vanquishing.
        We hunch in corners, untraceable breaths.
        The trees

                      tribute us for our stillness———
Muslims with a cityscape, shots ringing,
a trespasser older than time in their chests.
Did they hear

my aunt sobbing over tapped
phones on her way to buy lahm as the towers [　　]?
*Are you close to the [　　]? Is there a lot of [　　]?*
*Anyone listening?*

We find flags
          tooth-picked between our frames of the kaaba.
Each one whips a firework heat, red-blues consecrating
along our skin, smoke in our mouths, American touch.

My father gets a home security system——dark large
pupils always watching. *Just in case*, he says.
We speak in [     ],
          afraid they bugged the rooms,
imagining a device that hunts our [     ].
My parents
          turn down the music, lock the kids up,
place trackers in every car. I fall asleep with my ears:
growling K9s, laughter in the kitchen, click of a [     ].

## Assault

Ripping landslide of words—
dust's concealing flash

wrenches down across sodden lust.
Humans saddled and reaching,

reaching, as in sleep. An explosion
of utter midnight and struggle stands,

its maniacal afterthought looking
across the beast's darkened world.

Even so, memories of long-dead essentials
gleam above the dust, stride

upstream, huge and light,
into the frail world scrambling

in strange times for one
half-breath

of joy lying
dazed and waiting.

# This Thing Rising between Us

The fireman whose children
Carry flowers and ashes,
He could be my brother.

The young suicide bomber,
Dark-eyed and serious,
He could be my son.

The woman veiled, standing
Silent in the rubble of Kandahar
She could be me.

The old woman in the shelter
Rocks herself, repeats
Her words like a mantra,

I am alive, I am alive.

I, too, am alive

What shall I do now?

## No Bloodshed during Snowfall

*The snow dusted neighborhoods, Shiite and Sunni alike, faintly falling, as James Joyce wrote, like the descent of their last end, the living and the dead. . . . A flurry is a swift and passing joy.*
 —Associated Press, January 12, 2008

The long-haired Filipino kid with dolorous eyes
sits up front with me. Two more and a small Chinese girl,
Suk Li, called "Shirley," ride in back.
                                    We have feasted
on Lebanese food at Neomonde—kibi, tabooley, laban—
and studied together for hours at the NC Museum of Art:
Roman torsos, Egyptian heads, African masks,
Melanesian Pipes, a Wyeth house, an O'Keeffe church,
early American portraits. "Those men," Shirley pointed
to three be-wigged people on the wall, "look like—
your Founding Fathers?" The black security guard
has taken our laughing picture before a mobile
with flowers and butterflies shaped like a fighter plane.
                                    Now the radio says
that it has snowed in Baghdad after eighty years. We pass
a row of crabapple trees blooming pink in January.
*A flurry is a swift and passing joy.*

21

# A Finger

After most of the bodies were hauled away
and while the FBI and Fire Department and NYPD
were still haggling about who was in charge, as smoke cleared,
the figures in Tyvek suits came, gloved, gowned, masked,
ghostly figures searching rubble for pieces of people,
bagging, then sending the separate and commingled remains
to the temporary morgue set up on site.
This is where the snip of forefinger began its journey.

Not alone, of course, but with thousands of other bits not lost
or barged off with the tonnage for sorting at the city landfill.
A delicate tip, burnt and marked "finger, distal" and sent over
to the Medical Examiner's, where forensic anthropologists
sorted human from animal bones from Trade Center restaurants,
all buried together in the Pompeian effect of incinerated dust.

The bit of finger (that might have once tapped text messages,
potted a geranium, held a glass, stroked a cat, tugged
a kite string along a beach) went to the Bio Lab
where it was profiled, bar-coded, and shelved in a Falcon tube.
Memorial Park, that is to say: the parking lot behind the ME,
droned with generators for the dozens of refrigerated trucks
filling with human debris, while over on the Hudson at Pier 94
families brought toothbrushes or lined up for DNA swabbing.

As the year passed, the unidentified remains were dried out
in a desiccation room—humidity pumped out, heat raised high—
shriveled, then vacuum sealed.

                              But the finger tip had
a DNA match in a swab from her brother. She was English.
Thirty years old. She worked on the 105th floor of the North Tower.
The *Times* ran a bio. Friends posted blogs. Her father
will not speak about it. Her mother planted a garden in Manhattan.
In that garden is a tree. Some look on it and feel restored.
Others, when the wind lifts its leaves, want to scream.

# September 11th (Tuesday Schedule)

First period I sit in a high school study room beside
my ninth grade student, a genius, bullied the five years
I've known him. He's lashed out again at his tormentor.
This is my domain, the shame and hurt of schoolchildren.

Sweat trickles down my sides with the effort to
*remain neutral, resist engagement,* be quiet. I work
with defiant children who can use time beside a kind adult
as an opening for combat. If I'm patient, their stories emerge.

On September 11th, the boy I listen to at 8:05 tells me
about his fight behind the school, tells me his brain
has turned into a computer, *a real computer.*
What thoughts will assault him next?

The warning bell for second period rings. In the narrow
hallway, silent students mass around a TV on a rolling cart.
I ask a girl to tell me what I'm seeing on the screen,
but she can hardly pull her gaze away to speak.

Running to the parking lot, briefcase banging, *our children's
schools blown up, my husband dead on a street, my parents
on fire*—but my husband is home, we call the kids'
schools, our parents. I drive to my next student, shaking.

I visit the angry third grader who can't read. She tells me
her red hair makes girls hate her. She's only compliant
when she dictates a story or when I time her furious runs
around the building, her auburn ponytail flying.

In today's story, a princess is born speaking a language
no one else speaks, not even the king and queen.
The princess runs away from the castle. She cries
because she's alone in the forest, until, at long last,

the lonely princess meets World Woman,
who greets her in the language no one else understands.
World Woman teaches the princess everything she knows,
then leads her back home. I pray her home is safe.

I leave my redheaded princess to the mercies of the palace
and take my place in a new world order, where what I know
about children, their battles and losses, does me no good,
a kingdom where ashes settle and flags blossom.

## Curtain Time

The Israel Philharmonic tunes.
Taut gut screech achieves
a common chord. Audience
arid whispers spin as bows bounce
into a comfortable music.
Jerusalem's elite nestle
in sequined gowns, Windsor knots.

Another Bush war shorts harmony.
Scuds toward Tel Aviv. Sirens
by the sea wall. Children clutch,
bustle into sealed rooms
in the blistered city's bowel.

To offer order where none reigns,
Isaac Stern emerges from a crease
of the scarlet curtains, armed
with a short Bach piece. Elegant
notes calm terror's surge.

Like bloated frogs, the string section
takes the lead. Strapped gasmasks
and tuxedos; the audience too,
goggles under baubles, cut in
to soft flesh, tousle hairdos.

Overpowering air-raid sirens,
Stern in command continues,
fluent passages exorcising evil.
His crisp tails swaying, he defies
the threat; performs his duty.

Fired by a brave insanity,
his fury stands firm. Across
the desert, American Patriot
missiles bursting in air,
artillery pounding sand dunes

to dust. Shrapnel will be
left to rust. Even on this
Saturday night, Bach
cannot clean the bloody Tigris.
No stagnant breeze can

flush the caustic smell.
Violins have no coda to peace
even as the *All Clear* sounds.
Gasmasks removed,
placed at arm's length.

Imminent ground-war rumored,
but tonight a temporary peace.
The orchestra spared, still
the birthplace of civilization
weeps. Bows up,
Stern's wand resumes. Midnight
sandstorm delivers the psalter
of Adam's bleached rib.

# Threat

Through crushed August grass
a child's gray shoelace tugs itself,
its tiny pebble of a head triangular,
a wedge, therefore venomous.
Laced through a sneaker's eyelets,
it nips a finger, a tiny prick. One
worries in the mountains. Goldenrod
seeds our heads with bites from some
insect. Meanwhile upright red rod
flowers burn for hummingbirds.
Portable shield on his back, a turtle
labors, feels with splayed paws, shows
off his orange splotched arms, leopard
patterned, bright as marigold, as
oranges bowled all along the railroad,
where a supermarket truck, pulling
across, got its back half sheared off.
Cop cars beetled up and down the road.
A boy on vacation by a lake said, "Let's
go in," but my husband refused. The
boy, and another who went after him,
drowned. Each night of his childhood
my husband dreamed it, woke just
before dying. One's death is the period
that ends the sentence. In Cairo
on the sidewalk men link arms, like
paper dolls I cut as a kid. All at once
a waterfall of bodies bows to Mecca.

## Earthlog: Final Entry

Early in the voyage
we discovered idolatry among the passengers.
We tried to let them alone because we thought they needed it
but it's a small ship
and even with our guidance system its course through Chaos
has been erratic
and they threatened destruction      in our names
though there was no jealousy among us.

We let them act out
their ceremonies and rituals to us
In the name of the names they called us
                              and they died in each other's arms
"honkies niggas papists kikes wops mohammedans"
died on the altars in their minds
                    snarling eyes
                    fists locked
                    on crosses, manifestos, texts they called "sacred"

We wept
and comforted each other
                    when they tore out the hearts of their sons
                    to please us
ashamed to be prophets and gods to fools

Now the sons of devils and slaves watch the stars
and navigate well
and call themselves "Men."

It's a relief to feel not needed.
          Our deaths or retirements
          may be imminent

## Katy

After the first plane,
Katy phoned her brother.
She was safe, in *another* building.

They were evacuating. DJ thought
she had said *the other building*—
the South Tower—crashed into

by United Flight 175 at 9:03,
moments after the line went dead.
That's all Katy's mother, my sister,

Marie, could tell me when I called.
All we had to cling to:
a single syllable, separating *another*

from *other*, negligible, mere nuance;
but, in this case, the difference
between escape and incineration—

a seam notched for her in the secret ether,
should she stumble into it,
to pass through unharmed.

To cast wider our search,
Marie and I tuned to different networks,
watching for Katy among the fleeing hordes.

They had talked the night before
about what she'd wear to her client meeting:
a brown suit, a black bag; her black hair

was shorter since last I'd seen her.
All day I peered into the TV—punching
the cordless: Katy's office, home, cell,

office, home, cell, over and over—scanning
faces unraveling diabolically
like smoldering newsreels, smeared

with hallucinatory smoke and ash.
They came in ranks, wave upon wave,
leagued across the avenues:

the diaspora into John's Apocalypse.
Those still on their feet staggered.
Others lay in the street snarled

in writhing weirs of fire-hose.
The firmament had been napalmed:
orange-plumed, spooling black. Volcanic stench.

Somewhere beyond the screen,
inside that television from which we all, that day,
received, like communion, the new covenant,

for all time, was my niece in her brown suit
and new haircut, her purse—outfitted
for her seventh day in Manhattan,

her fourth day at the World Financial Center,
six days past her twenty-second birthday.
I would spy her, coax her back to us

through the TV's lurid circuitry
into my living room. Our perfect girl,
my princess—she had lost her shoes—

wandering the skewered heart of the future—
finally arrived, black-hooded, afire,
eerily mute—toward the Upper East side:

a bus, a shared cab with an old man
who befriended her, then barefoot blocks
and blocks to her apartment on 89th Street

where she dialed her parents and announced
with the sacrificial modesty of saints
that she had made it home.

## Going South

They'd made the start from North Washington,
passed through Walla Walla,
Milton-Freewater,
I joining there the busload,
and God but they were without.

So little!
Blankets and baskets and the Greyhound creaking
baskets and blankets and a cardboard box
glasses and rubber boots
knotted brown hands
and everything and hope on board, in short.

Up and down hills:
Weston, Athena, Pendleton,
and I recall somewhere between he looked at her,
turning half-round his seventy-wintered
and rheumatic head
and thrilling spastic-like, jerking words
because of February cold,
to California-or-bust, his partner, wife, said,
"Mother, I can feel it. It's getting warmer
already,"
said, "We're in Oregon now, you know.
It's quite a difference."

I couldn't wince,
nor could I choose to ponder
on the heart's brown moment
with twelve above outside and cold feet, too.
I knew it wasn't really getting warmer,
mountains ahead and open land
with gusts of wind soon up
the Columbia River Gorge to the right; the Bend
southmountain country ditto.

"My God!" I said inside
"How can they prop this poor act up—
this poor pretense at hope."
But they had to and they knew and I knew
and I wanted
        with them
wanted with them,
but knew it wasn't getting any warmer,
except, perhaps,
the region of the heart.

# The Boy in the Ambulance

He sits alone
in a bright orange seat
next to the first aid kit.

No tears.
No bandages.
Only the weary stare
of a five-year-old
painted with ash
and dried blood.

Bare feet dangling,
he owns only his body,
the dirt-stained shorts
and T-shirt
that bear the marks
of the hands
that saved him.

Pulled from
the mangled floor
of his apartment
barrel-bombed
in the middle of the night
by an enemy
he'll never see,
he waits,
like a passenger
on a plane
or a bus,
the lull of calm
before departure.

No news of his parents,
siblings, neighbors.
All we can report
for sure this night
from the ancient city
of Aleppo
is that one child lives
in the back
of an ambulance
where it is safe,
for now.

Author's Note: Five-year-old Omran Daqneesh, his three siblings
and parents were rescued from the rubble after an airstrike hit the
family's apartment building in the northern Syrian city of Aleppo
on Aug. 17, 2016. Omran suffered head injuries and was later
discharged from a nearby hospital. Syrian government forces have
been fighting a bitter and bloody civil war with a series of rebel
groups since 2011 for control of the country. The war has displaced
millions of Syrians and killed nearly 500,000 people, according to
humanitarian agencies.

## A Stone Falling, a Falling Stone

I am not afraid to fall.
Drop me from a tower & I
simply hit the earth.  Hold on
to me, I am earth still.
I want to fall, it is the first
dream for me.  And the earth
my drum that I play.

A stone falling, a falling stone.
Whether I burn or not—
that's beside the point.
The point, this:
when the earth
makes a stone
the sky still fathers it.
When the earth makes a stone,
it's made for falling.

I am not afraid to fall.

# The Day after the Coup

A green wall of jungle blazes outside
the window of the English Department room.
The professors wear their uniforms today,
creased and rumpled from being folded in trunks.
In stifling heat, we're made to stand at attention
like laurel leaves shrunk stiff in a cold snap.
Stocky soldiers in camouflage fatigues
weave between us. The sergeant grunts sharp
questions. Like a schoolmaster, he jabs at papers
with the grooved steel tip of his bayonet.

Later, we take chicken and *somtaam* salad,
to three teachers in jail. Kwaam sits
cross-legged on cement in striped
prison shorts, his shirt draped over his neck
like a towel. Purple bruises shine
through the sweat on his chest.
We pass packets of yellow papaya
between the bars. His house burned down
last night. *Professor*, he whispers to me,
*how do you like our Thai prisons?*

Professor Som's still missing. *I hope he stays
in the mountains*, Suthep says. It's night.
We talk on his porch as frogs whistle
love calls in the canals. He's my boss, the newly
appointed dean. Moths fly into the candlelight
and fall, splashing, in a wide water pan
he set on the table to catch them. Turned low,
his police radio murmurs about students barricaded
in a Bangkok university, fighting tanks.

*Communist dogs*, he growls. *They have guns
in their rooms, make trouble for everyone.*

I ask what will happen. He shrugs.
*The soldiers will kill them.* I take the pan
and pour the moths onto the ground,
set it back on the table again. One flops over,
legs grasping at air. Others lie drowned
on the grass. Sutape says good night,
pinches out the flame with his thumb.

## The Cyclist

I watch
as planes circle and slice
the planes of two tall towers
then call Dad
*Where's Michael?*
The boy we grew up with
who still maintains contact.
The boy who grew up to fly airplanes.
Later we'll learn he was in the air
circling, being diverted
to a safe place to land.

Fifteen years later
I'm out for coffee on the morning of Dad's funeral
and I see Michael cycling
weaving in and out of parked cars
hands free
balancing and tipping precariously
lost
in his thoughts.

He's lost contact with his siblings
wife and children
still occasionally connected with Dad
but doesn't attend his funeral
At the cemetery he stands at a distance
his bike propped against an oak
then like a phantom is gone without notice
before the empty hearse pulls away.

That evening my family gathers for beers
and reminiscing and the rumors
of our friend's constant cycling
all over town, all hours of the day.

There's little relief in
*There but for the grace of God . . .*
for those who carry
> *it could have been my office tower*
> *it could have been my flight*
> *it could have been my passengers and crew*

We leave the taproom as a cyclist glides by.
He smiles and waves.
I watch the steady spin of reflectors recede into the night
like blinking lights of an airplane
aiming toward a safe
and familiar place to land.

# For Okra

I'd never seen so green a green
before, so lean
those tender pods
I stopped and bought

when I knew for certain you were
not on that plane.
Trish, what would my
selfish life have

been? But no—come get some okra
now. I've dredged and
fried it. Just the
way you like it.

# Western Chant

Whenever I Abu Ghraib with you
against the grout in the shower, or take
the dog—part collie, part pinscher—for
a short Abu Ghraib to foul the avenue,
or even drink from the bowl made
in heat-resistant Abu Ghraib, I often think
of Abu Ghraib and how, from here
on out, whether I read a book of porn
published in Abu Ghraib or look
closely at fashion in *The Times*
with stoic models from the thin runways
of Abu Ghraib, things will be marked
by those photos from Abu Ghraib.
But with time, I'll relax, let my guard
down, and focus on the small Abu
Ghraib of the backyard, and the food
we prepare being charred at Abu Ghraib,
and the clothes we wear or strip off,
the teeth we chew with, filled with
the silver mined in Abu Ghraib,
and the miners themselves, little men
with a penchant for being down
the darkest shafts with canaries
from the provinces of Abu Ghraib,
everything, even after years, becomes
laced with Abu Ghraib, something
the dark dogs sniff out at Abu Ghraib,
and my face, even when I see it
with my eyes closed, is stamped
Abu Ghraib, like a Made in USA tag,
and I lie back and see myself in
Abu Ghraib, first as the happy handler
yanking the chain, then as the black and white
man with the studded leash around his

neck, and I sense the small ray of
piercing light at the end of a long colonnade
is burning a hole, even if I do as I say
and don't move or blink, and it burns through
the skin and my shiny organs of bloat,
until it reaches the fortress-like Abu Ghraib
in the center of me. That's the point
at which I hear and begin to chant Abu Ghraib,
Abu Ghraib, to the Olympic music
of USA, USA, Abu Ghraib, USA.

## With Each Stitch

September's sun lights up Lamb's Ear,
red begonia, chrysanthemum.
A weed I have never seen before stitches
its way out of the dark furrows, chokes
the pansies, and winds around the
sunflowers' tall stems.

The phone rings—*Have you heard?*
my daughter asks. *Turn on your TV.*

My hands cut with sharp scissors and place
piece by piece. I press the pedal hard.
The needle pierces the fabric.
Stitches leave their marks.
One shape after another, a blaze of colors
across the quilt. Yellow iris appear. Green
leaves grow with each stitch.

I walk out into the garden.
No longer in the light, Lamb's Ear fold
into themselves. Knees on the ground,
I dig the earth. Cool dirt falls through my fingers.

The phone rings—my son—*I'm safe.*

# After the AfterMATH: 9x11=23

(The Second Assassination of Abraham, Martin, John and Bobby)

*The United States themselves are essentially the greatest poem.*
—Walt Whitman

Everything begins at the beginning. Therefore, the tragedy of Gotham looks
all the way back to Y1K +92y = $\frac{1776}{13}$ stars divided by 13 faded stripes

draped over dead noise $\frac{now}{yesterday}$ divided by $\frac{tomorrow}{if}$ it comes

again into that blue Gotham City morning of remembering how civil a Civil
War refuses to be. Y1K+800+65y divided by 2 = 1 Nation
under God

speed = $\frac{distance}{time}$ divided by $\frac{time}{speed}$ = Times Square clock stopped

but, still, light travels in a straight line. Tyrone was still asleep on a Central
Park bench. Nancy was standing in front of the front-office coffee pot. Tom
was driving into the City, late for work. Stefano was putting on his makeup.

An Al-Qaeda trigonometry of right triangles turned abruptly left and left all

seats empty. -2 World Trade Center Towers + a field adjacent Stonycreek

Township, PA + the Pentagon = 4 airline flight plans changed in mid-flight.

So $\frac{N}{O}$ = no x $\frac{zero}{zero}$ at Ground level Zero = $\frac{Man}{Hat}$ = Tan black billowing

black smoke billowing into the choking history of ... Y1K 941 $\frac{FD}{R}$ still

with us, still smoking a pipe. $\frac{December}{Pearl\ Harbor}$ "Nothing to fear but fear itself."

Raj had just missed his train. Cora Castro was stuck in LA traffic. Allyson, breast feeding her new baby. The captain has turned off the seat belt sign.

4 billowing black smokes attributable to the angry   distorted   distribution of   <u>Osama Bin</u>  x  4  FLTs of         compressed refried confusion
          Laden

divided by   <u>Jesus</u>  inverted without warning to  <u>Allah</u>  x   9x11= 23.
        Allah                               Jesus

When velocity is constant, displacement varies directly with the names of Mary—Jacqueline—Ethel—Coretta Scott crying the same 4 tears over again.

Taniesha was dropping off the kids at day care. Sydney, asleep on a pallet. The captain has turned off the...Aabdar was waiting for the bank to open.

Simultaneous quadratic explosion on National TV, I was drinking a second cup of coffee, a break between teaching university classes. Liberty, herself

resigned into the statue of.................................................<u>What</u>
                                                    If

AK47 + 1= AK48 + 2 = 50 United States of confusion lower at half-mast or mass greater than and/or equal to the sum of static in the pockets of 19 boys. 5+14 or 9+10 or 7+11 or 17 + 2 or 16 + 3 or 18 + 1 = all 19 box-cut boxes cut not to fit underneath the seat or in the overhead compartment. 19 dead Muslim boys, 19 DOA cigarette boys. 19 dead boys + 4 dead flights diverted =                             9 x 11= 23.

NBC CBS ABC FOX BBC 93. 5 FM divided by <u>C</u> =                CNN
                                          N square

September 11, 2001, a working-class Tuesday morning, uninvited thunder multiplied -1,492 divided into1,776 stars, then add 2,001 stripes =<u>1u and 1i</u>
                                                     9x11

Live from Ground Zero, New York City, "This is Bryant Gumbel, I'm down on 59th and 5th, where are you?" Miss Jones was taking morning attendance. Oliver Joe was drunk, waiting for the liquor store to open. Ed, walking home

after night shift when he saw the smoke. Billy Ray was tending his livestock. Ava Batts was still fast asleep, still dreaming. The captain has turned off the...


Every report, the exact same, 3,000 dead. Light travels in a straight line. 4 lines of morning angry air, no easy despair spilled onto FAA flight plan of...

30,000 feet and still climbing. You are now free to move about the cabin. In case of an emergency,... your seat cushion can be used as a flotation device.


Note: Word fractions should be read as: Ex.　$\dfrac{\text{Jesus}}{\text{Over}}$
Allah

# Safe

I knew no one who perished.
For that I am grateful.
My nephew had moved from the city a year ago.
My friends lived or worked blocks away from Ground Zero.
One watched from her office the small bodies leaping.
Another stepped onto the street as the second plane circled.
Out of the subway another climbed into a sky of glass falling.
The scrolls of their e-mails continued for days.

Again and again I try not to imagine myself onto either plane,
the continent stretching before me,
out there on the edge of it, sun just beginning to rise.
Seat belts off.
Scent of fresh coffee. The rattle of carts.

Here nothing flies into my windows but birds.
They have lain in my daughter's palms,
pressed to her chest for the warmth of her beating heart,
until their broken-necked bodies grew cold,
and she looked up at me, as if asking, What now?
And I answered, Now go wash your hands.

# Cataclysm

*Writers' group: my house tomorrow morning.*
                    —Message from Joy Acey, September 10, 2001


                    I.


When the twin towers in Manhattan crumple,
we are at the house of Joy, five women
gathered this blue-sky morning to consider
the power of words.  Wordless,
we watch, as what cannot happen
does:  those massive definitions of the skyline
transform to cascades of roiling foam
like dingy showers of disconnected syllables,
a gibberish of steel, stone,
plastic,  paper,  glass,
flesh and bone.
Beyond the television screen, beyond
the windowed wall, two finches
placidly work the feeder,
their luminous gold multiplied
by a shaft of September sunlight.
In Manhattan, trucks, streets, air,
fleeing people, quivering ruins
coalesce: one shuddering moonscape
shrouded in ash,
one grim hue.  Worn
by the severe preponderance of gray,
we lift eyes to exuberant greens
of Carolina forest, underscored
by the scarlet splash of cardinals,
the blurs of hummingbirds.

## II.

That night, in sleep, unbidden images
persist.  The Pentagon's perfectly angled structure
broken, blazing. A jumble of plane and persons
smashed into Pennsylvania woods.
Manhattan: from one pristine tower,
a sudden bloom flares orange-gold,
igniting in mid-flight hapless sparrows.
From clouded windows, workers, just arrived
to start their nine-to-five, are spurred
to final awful choices:
plunge scores of floors, embracing wind
and swift, final impact, alternative
to furious fire and unbreathable air.
A metal bird appears, then disappears
into the second tower—magic,
now you see it, now you don't (how
did they do that? who? and why?)—
then flame erupts, another brilliant blossom,
sends smoke surging like prayers
to the helpless sky.

III.

Images and words; words and images.
Compelled, we hear, view
words and images, images and words,
grope, hope to discover something
sufficiently firm to shift
our newly-tilted world
into familiar form, click fuzzy edges
into accustomed focus.
We fill chaotic hours
uncluttering desks and cabinets,
re-ordering closets, ruthlessly uprooting
the tangle of horsenettle and stiltgrass
that threatens the marigolds.
Scrubbing filth from the bird-bath, we pour
glistening water to the brim. We mow
our sick friend's lawn, are grateful for
the mower's happy clatter. We offer
money, messages, blood.
Nothing
suffices.

# Tony Writes to Say He's Alive

September, and the morning
rainfreshed. Rises
from the goldening birch thicket
steam and cricket-shimmer,
as though leaves and dirt
both speak and breathe.
Burns softly through
exhalations of earth and river,
the sun, not yet
shining, but seeping
into each fat red leaf, each pink rosette
of a begonia in a round blue pot.
Droplets fill with light
and light blooms
from darkened places:
a crevice in a flower, a new
cupped leaf. So
slow and sure, so
long past daybreak,
so welcome. So,
even ashes
even bones ground down
to dust must moisten, must
grow soft and still.
Must be penetrated by rain,
then by warmth, then
by rain again.

Must some morning
rise up, green.

# Contractions: September 11, 2001

I wake to the rumble of tiny kicks
as your father's palm cups my belly.
We talk of you and laugh, guess
when you are coming. Today,
on your grandmother's birthday? Or tomorrow?
Can you wait until you are due?

Dreams still intact, we move to the couch,
your dad turns on his laptop:
WORLD TRADE CENTER UNDER ATTACK!
*What's this, a joke?* He snaps
on the TV and the first tower
disintegrates into dust.

Your father's face turns to ash.
*I know people in there.* On his phone,
8:05 a.m., a message from the North Tower, 51st floor.
He tries to call back. *All circuits are busy.*

For hours we watch the tapes
of planes slicing into steel buildings,
roiling clouds of gray
swallowing city streets,
wide-eyed, soot-faced survivors.
I hold your father's hand,
envision smoke-filled
stairwells, cell phones ringing,
soles of shoes melting. Your father's friend
made it out alive.

Two months earlier,
when the doctor probed my cervix,
she said, *You're dilated!* and sent me
to the hospital. A nurse strapped a belt

around my abdomen. *This is labor!*
I imagined a blue-skinned baby under a glass dome,
a tangle of wires, huff of ventilator
pumping air into fishlike lungs.

Your father called from London.
*What does this mean?* He caught
the next flight home. The doctor ordered
bed rest until the danger was over.
Now darkness falls like cinders.
I think of cool sheets and morning innocence,
how we daydreamed of your pink face,
wrinkled skin, damp hair
in curlicues around your head.

The doctor said if you came early
you'd be covered in vernix caseosa,
a pale, cheesy substance
that's hard to wipe off,
but nothing like the soot of this day.

# Grace's Quilt

Sun was shining that time
I shuffled to Grace's house
Vast homeland of pieced cloth
We sat stitching together.
  *from California to the New York Island*


Needles up and down through
Stars and spangled banners
Needles dipping, diving through
Layers of cloth and batting.
  *All around me a voice was sounding*

Grace's quilt filled the room
TV in a far corner
With planes beheading
Twin Towers spitting toxic dust
  *And the rocket's red glare, the bombs bursting in air*

Sirens from the box split our ears
Showers of dust covering
Men, women, and children.
Rivers of tears flow down our threads.
  *And the wheat fields waving and the dust clouds rolling*

Grace cried—Stitch!
Stitch this country together
Our fingers flew from California
East to Oklahoma and Texas.
  *From the redwood forest to the Gulf Stream waters*

Grace thumped her thimble on the table.
Damn oil curse she shouted!
Oil curse, Grace?
God knows I would love Saudi oil gold.
  *Saw below me that golden valley*

But who would want foreigners trooping around
Grace spat?  This land is my land!
  *This land was made for you and me*

# The Attending

Let us, in this time of bitterest lament,
Go awhile apart and meditate
And reverently attend the ancestral choir
Of prophets, sages, founders of the state,
Who lend us strength and solace when the world is rent
And everywhere besieged with fire.

Let us linger, as we may, within the grove
And hear those voices in the heat of day
Speak like gentle winds stirring the silence
Softly in their never-ceasing play
Of loving variations on the theme of love
And weary descant against violence.

For we are nothing without the ones who came before,
They who with palette, loom, and graceful pen
And sculpted stone, with treatise and debate
Built up our world and built it up again
When it was brought to rubble by incendiary war
And the towering, sword-blade flames of hate.

And let us join with them in spirit by going to
Their words and deeds that make our history
A matter of some pride, if we will know
The best of it, forgoing vanity
And boast and doing calmly what we ought to do,
As they did then, a world ago.

## Every Which Way Holiness

the diameter of the love song
is about an inch, the size of
the speaker mounted in the car door
but the diameter expands to five
inches when it fills an average
fist-shaped heart, and the diameter
of two hearts listening to the same
song in a car parked on the Blue
Ridge Parkway under a June moon
is large enough to hold dreams
of the young couple starting to compose
a life together on the western side
of a state that makes a fist
to defend itself against anyone
who loves the wrong god, the wrong
woman or man, but the love that rises
from the Subaru travels from mountains
to sea, making the diameter of a circle
that includes every roadside shrine, minaret,
cross, prayer rug, pipe, sacred scroll—all
the ritual objects and worshippers facing
every which way in the directions of holiness,
and the chemists and bankers and coders, whatever
their disbeliefs as the fist tightens
and releases, tightens and releases, every
day a face to fear, a basket to fill
with lettuce and corn, every hour
its own light, a flash, a glimmer, a brilliant sky
planes cross, carrying who knows
what hatred, what love to its final destination

# Come to Devour

The distant field, the longing, the slow lope
of the long gone, see how it clears the slope
and stretches, the distance burning. An Loc
burning, the jungle enlightened and not.

Very lights move through time like particles
through hearts. What more do they carry, close parts?
What do we? What do we not. Dark matter.
Dark matters to the soldier in the field,

the wolf pacing the verges, eyes like ours,
or so we like to think. Hours pass. We make
war. We do. We make the fictional beasts
of the field and the jaws that bring them down.

The long arm, the cuffs, the links, the glancing
blow of memory or something like it.

## Is This the Best We Can Do?

*Idiot wind. . .blowing down the back roads headin' south. . .*
*It's a wonder that you still know how to breathe.*
> —Bob Dylan, "Idiot Wind," *Blood on the Tracks*

Turn wonderful air
into a hurricane of haze—
Turn landscape and vistas
into pictures painted for the blind—
Fill pink lungs of children
with black space—
Make soot we breathe
surreal salt in the food of film noir,
for profit and at any price.

From a pile of coal
make heat—
Make light
from a hill of peat—
From hellbent    to heartache
hookers of energy    in bed with the rich;
the blood of the poet in a Blue Ridge ditch,
for profit and at any price.

Stay cool in the face of fire—
The gift of mankind:
an eternal pyre—
For profit and at any price.
  Hands and head in a vice.
  Denying Nature not two times, but thrice.
  Fanning the flames of dry ice.
  Use poison in food and calling it spice.
  For what profit? What price?

Take transfusions of blood in the air—
Honor madmen and government not really there,
who call the rain "sunshine"    and the circle square,
for profit and at any price.

Only an idiot
would try to make love to the wind.
Would inhale oxygen and call it $CO_2$.
Or think sun and moon
would come from some Yahweh living in another place.
Would kiss the lips of bombs and call them sweet.
Or move their home to somewhere in outer space.
This    is grace?
This    the human race?

# Idol

O arts people, the Smithsonian preserves,
      in the archives, a safe, squashed
under a World Trade Center tower.

     A metal lump, flesh-beige,
crumpled, dented, furrows
       swerving like sand dunes

or alluvia, it still holds foreign
      currency, brightly
colored paper money, orange, purple,

      ripped, wadded, pictures
of presidents and heroes,
       twisted, cauterized into the seams.

Half a red ten dollar bill from Aruba.
      Who'd attack Aruba?
A compressed, singed

      stack of two dollar bills
from Barbados Central Bank.
      Five hundred thousand Turkish lire.

The crate it sits in stinks of disinfectant,
      ancient smoke.
Impossible to tell,

      from the pattern of the folds
—like an Oldenburg, "Thumbprint,
      Enlarged"—the angle

of the blow.  Every way
          at once?  Photographer,
hurry, no one's watching, take

          this object, worthless, holy,
through a scarlet filter.  Make
          a statement.  Say

it smells of us, our dust, blood,
          countless corpses,
soldiers, citizens, curled, like

          seeds, in spring mud.
We'll supply the future
          cultures,

stumbling from clump
          to clump,
scavenging,

          bidding.

# Once-ese

Inténtalo otra vez pero a
hora en English because there were
two the towers two the years
in Atlanta two the country and
you both cut in half the shock of
seeing the world collapse you never
know you barely know what's going to
happen a step before you fall
it's not my fault why do they hate
us your flawless laws you saw what
happened but now if you look back
if you looked up the towers fold
into the sky I saw then once
I saw them twice I saw them gone
I saw the other side I saw
the void avoid the flags because
the flags where I come from were not
the sign of one oh well they were
the flags of one imposed upon
the pluribus give me no one
so Lisa raised stars and stripes
over my door it was a strike
my door shut up que tú no entien
des oh yes I know it took us
time to understand there will be
more planes that will crush down upon
the common folks the common fog
around the truth just not your own
just no I don't I don't I post
ed a sign that read proud to be
an alien después a simple
word change again and again and
a country cries power of pride
powder of pier powder of dust

dios dos two two towers twin mo
ments in time but master Dōgen
says—I heard it read by Gary—
the blue mountains walk the towers
falling the flags arising half
mast knock-knock who is it oh honey
it's I it's ICE open the door
police the kick mid-night raid half
across the world it's cut in half
I'm not from here yo soy Joa
quín me quedo aquí an AK-
47 the world became
a darker place a darkened sky

# Twenty Years Later

I remember a school
of silver sky fish shimmering
against a clear blue backdrop.

My first thought was: *This is how
vultures circle over a wounded animal,
waiting for the inevitable.*

But they didn't glide as if at home.
They cut and banked more like frantic
sharks when blood is in the water.

Blood was in the air that day.
Even before I knew, I knew
something was wrong.

My highway ride to morning class
was trafficless for once. The only sound
was tire rubber humming on asphalt.

Parking spaces were plentiful and
I wondered if I'd missed a memo:
"Take the day off; go for a ride."

When a student parked nearby
I asked, "What's with all the planes?"
and she told me.

Glancing back to that moment
and every moment since we huddled
around a small teachers' lounge tv

and watched a second plane spear
the second tower, knowing we
were under attack, knowing planes

swarmed overhead as someone sorted
friend from foe, I wonder now if we
will ever know the difference again.

## Message to the Unborn

A sign saddles the chain
across the strip mine road:
Do Not Enter.
Feldspar exposed as upturned petticoats,
woods still in shock,
blackberry seeds, carried
by the faith of birds,
are the first to claw
the edge of newly impoverished soil.
Anything battered offers
what might be liked more
when diverse forest
was not good enough,
forsaken for rock exploded from beneath.
Still, there is always a price to pay,
even while cobbler
bubbles purple over a browning crust
or a timber rattler stumbles into the clearing,
unable to discern, amid thick berries,
a bird from a small hand.

Eventually, black birch
stamps out the blackberry stand.
A few white pines foot in.
A vertical mine shaft
engages a water table,
spills over; bleeds rust into the creek.
A horizontal shaft caves in
under the pressure of dairy cows,
and another surfaces open as a gaping whale
outside a potter's shed -
adapted for broken shards.
Newly dug wells bubble with arsenic.
Stems of the invasive birch are sweet

for chewing during walks,
but heed my words:
never will the quiet notes of a Solomon's seal
lilt here again.

The delicate microcosm of humus,
refined by fungi symbiotic with forest roots
into the nutrients and exact pH,
yield orchids so specialized
their pollination requires
one specific insect.
Farther below, blue and green gems and quartzite
stretch fingers of illumination through bedrock
with a magnetism generated
by planets and stars shifting millions of years
into beauty as balm for such truth.

Generations away,
no white trillium
will be allowed to offer its hope
against the charred forest floor.

So many people in the world,
souls leaping in quickly
to grasp the last opportunity to live,
born into suffering.
This is not living.
I want you to live,
to taste huckleberries on your walk,
to smell the negative ions on the cliff
above the roar of the river gorge
with the feeling of peace pulling you back.

I want to give you more
than what I came with,
but the acid sky and
metallic ocean will burn
the earth down to more darkness
than a lonely mine shaft could ever dream up.
After the paintings and books are gone,
can your souls
invent an art to make it worth starting over?
Listen while poetry still
circles you like a moon.
Know that you are the ones
I have always spoken to.
I wanted you to find hidden places
that you would love—
inside rooms of rhododendron
or where miniature yellow lady's slippers
grow in limestone-rich soil.
Know that I love you,
that I want to meet you,
and that I do not want to bear this cruel message:
*Do Not Enter.*

## That Tuesday Morning

I thought we lived in Mayberry—
our town as quiet and friendly and safe—
and Western North Carolina seemed a world away
from New York City.
Yet it didn't seem so distant
that Tuesday morning in September
when the horror filled our TV screens
and started our telephones ringing
with the news.
My mother called and said,
"Did you see what happened?"
and I could hear the fear in her voice.
"Where will they hit next?" we wondered
and found ourselves looking at the sky.
My community college students were agitated that night,
thinking we might be targeted.
I was grateful for the normality of work that day,
but hesitant to be away from my husband and baby.
The world changed that Tuesday morning—
our security and complacency gone.
Suddenly Mayberry was an illusion,
and we couldn't see how life
would ever be the same.

# Silence

Yates was cutting the lawn, a simple task
he made gracious, with swirls instead of lanes.
He stopped to say hello.
And because we always talked, this yard man
and I, about books, and flowers, and the names
of Southern trees, so strange to me,
because we always lingered to smile, to say a quick
hello, to set up lunch for another time, I said,
"You must get to a TV. Something terrible has happened."

I depended, that day, on the visual, for words eluded me.
The screen in the Student Union, in front of my classroom,
had shown a plane flying toward a skyscraper
and smoke, grey and black, billowing toward a blue sky
and I remembered thinking,
*Who is shooting that film?*
Is there CCTV on the buildings nearby?
No words. No words to tell Yates that this was
the beginning of the end of the world.

We never talked about that day, Yates and I.
What was there to say?
Someone had televised their revolution
and the images needed no lyrics.
It was like the silence in my group on the bus
after our visit to Auschwitz.
All we could do was look out at the trees,
so strange to us, and the clouds, heavy, gray and black
hovering over us.

# In a Just and Miniature World

I watched the flames draw closer
my daughters begging the world for good sleep
in a just and miniature world.
Dropping them at their school doors
I half-listened to news as the first plane
hit the first tower fifteen hundred miles away.
I drove to my wife's hospital room
as the second plane hit the second tower
She signed her last will. I gave her a last kiss
in a just and miniature world.
I watched the flames draw closer
small fires on the Nebraskan horizon
as the brooding tv seemed half-alive
above a divine pulse of soft tubes
pinned to her arms and lost veins.
After our good friends had fled
a bright angel left her body
my daughters begging for good sleep
in a just and miniature world.

# This Whistling Is for You There in the Dark

*And, we are here as on a darkling plain*
*Swept with confused alarms of struggle and flight*
*Where ignorant armies clash by night.*
      —Matthew Arnold, "Dover Beach"

*Owls hoot to mark their territory; whistling is a contact call.*
      —Duncan Brown, Welsh naturalist

We gather near Afon Dwyfor at the moth trap
to see what the blue light has drawn from the dark.
What we call a moth, Duncan tells us,
is just one stage, the imago,
the final flowering of its univoltine life.
He scoops out each one, careful not to crimp a wing,
speaks its poet's name before freeing it:
small phoenix, common marble carpet,
Svenson's copper underwing, pink bardsallo.
The Latin names, he says, echo evolutionary orders,
categories constantly changing.

These days, nations seal their borders,
Israel, India, Afghanistan, Uzbekistan,
forgetting how taxonomies can blur.
When Tomahawk missiles gather, when six shooters
slip from their holsters, what hope
even for lovers, like you and me?
How can we hope to lay aside our weapons—
the gunmetal silence, the empty e-mail screen?

*Peter Howson's "The Morning After"*
*monoprint and oil on paper:*
A female inert on the edge of a bed,
back turned like a shield.
Her mate, escaped from the other side,
clawing the air with a hand no longer his.
Hunched over, he regurgitates
a scream. Blood shadows him.

His or hers?  Impossible to say.
His soft genitals surface in the Venice red.
Outside the window, a wide-bodied plane
hovers above a building only six stories high,
a patient lover stroking with its wing.
Duncan says most creatures mark their domains.
Owls hoot and swoop along the edge of night.
Even moths claim their spots of light.

Tonight when we flutter together in the dark,
no taxonomies, please. Call me *Yellow Brimstone*.
I'll name you *July Highflier*.
*Melyn y drain, esgynnwr Gorffenaf.*
Then watch while I trace a circle
of candlelight on the bed,
and, for this one hour, claim it mine
and yours.

# lifting veils

11 september 2001

I

it is a bloodstained horizon
whispering *laa illaha il-allah*
prelude to a balmy evening
that envelops our embrace
we stand reaching across
sands, waters, airs full of blood

in the flash of a distant storm
i see you standing on another shore
torn hijab
billowing towards an unnamed wind

we both wear veils
blood stained
tear stained
enshrouding separate truths

II

misty morning
teardrops of dust
choke and stain lips
that do not move
will not utter
it is a morning of shores
sea shadows that caress memory
of another time
another veil
another woman needing
reaching
lifting

### III

into your eyes i swam
searching for veils
to lift
to wrap
to pierce
dance with
veils that elude such mornings
veils that stain such lips
veils tearing like music

### IV

it is the covering of spirit
not the body
my hijab your hijab
connecting interweaving crawling snaking binding
into a sky that will not bend

## Every Child

That spring the headlines grieved:
*Lindbergh's Baby Kidnaped,*
a mourning cloak that settled heavy
across the shoulders of every neighborhood.
Our sky lowered itself to rebuke
tulips and hyacinths, to renounce
all green, all color,
and the late snow drifted lawns
like an infant's down bunting.

Why should I have expected my daughter
to contain her four-year-old squeals
at the hills' white-lofted magic?
The sled dragged forth, her pink knit cap,
the azalea's pink hope smothered
and struggling like the fists of babies;
our flowered Easter frocks
smothered under damp black wool,
the opened tomb no consolation
for a son's shallow grave.

But my child lived—you are here, Great-grandson—
and I turn these clippings over to you,
but can I turn over all my grief? Remember
that the thousands you can't conceive
are born singly—just one
stolen through a nursery window,
beneath a wave, before
the black mouth of a soldier's barrel,
and every mother knows
the loss of every child.

# Teaching

*Perhaps I can never achieve the last,*
*but that will be my attempt.* —Rilke (translation Bly)

That morning    maybe a radio play on PBR
filled the way to work.    WINGS kids, first hour.
Many familiar from juvie sessions,    here now,
attempting acclimation    in mainstream school.

We shared story, prepped,    encouraged confidence,
caught up late work, headed    down the hall to join our
second periods, regular classes.

Chair of English stopped me.
Quivering, crying, asked    could I take her classes, said
she couldn't teach, didn't know    what she would say to the kids.

Figured she was having a day,    joined our sessions together,
began. Twenty minutes in, PA,    principal announced maybe
we were at war, New York    attacked from air, bombed.

The kids laughed loudly thinking
was a joke, just like I thought    radio play on PBR, coming in.

Next, custodians came in, took    out our TVs, computers, left us
unwired to the bone. PA sounded    announcements, no
one allowed leave    for lunch hour.

It was then I recited Bly's Rilke, "I Live My Life in Growing Orbits,"
Berry, "The Peace of Wild Things,"    spoke of introspection, thought.
Began teaching practice—responding    to reaction with reason, finding
peace in calamity,    being thoughtful    —*when despair for the world*—
be-ing.

Deputized those, ordained all my    other classes that day, in four
other schools that week, all, as peace    ambassadors who helped their

families, communities, neighbors,     teachers, too, deal with reason,
with love, compassion, resisting     racism, reaction, fear—hate.

Throwing out the curriculum     for the next twelve bars
we wrote poems of peace,     clarity, demonstrated strength
of peace, care.

In the end they published     *Coming to Life*     their anthology
of coping through peace     as practice. Made themselves
honorable, deliberate, intentional.

One sixteen-year-old put in jail,     as an adult,     for not wanting
to greet Bush on the football     field, saying he felt like slapping
anyone who waged war.

From Viet Nam, he was,     his family perpetrated on by US,
over and over. He never came     back to school,     they wouldn't
give his location. And kids     from other classrooms     grew
racist, enlisted,     came home in     body bags.

# Remembering 9/11: Soon It Will Be Ten Years, Lines Written on Sept. 4, 2011

Now and then, during the last hour,
when I have glanced out the window,
the dove has been there, the same spot
on the same telephone wire,
a shade of gray, scarcely moving.
The color and the bird reminds
and doesn't remind of a day
when morning broke, from blue to gray.

The dove on the wire is alone.
Uncommon, and odd: every dove
I've seen before was with a mate.
And something else I'd seen comes back—
a wire stretched between the towers,
the aerialist walking it
back and forth, the marvel of mind
and skill and maybe luck that wind

or misstep hadn't plummeted
him headlong down through breathless air,
another singular being.
He chose to occupy his time
doing what he alone could do.
He took a more visible way
than most, who, also, every one,
have one life, one time, that's their own.

This early September Sunday,
so near to the day of the tenth
year, I pray for those whose bodies,
in desperate courage, not to burn
alive, plummeted; pray for all
who died; and hope for those suffering
loss and memory of loss, that they
have faith love did not die that day.

I look out the window. The dove
has gone, has flown. The words *mourning
dove* come to mind, and how, native
where accent sounded them alike,
as a boy I had wondered if
the bird's name wasn't *morning dove*.
Now, both feelings are connecting:
I mourn; I'm glad it is morning.

# Going Back

before September 11

Hold to the interlude
when innocence fulfilled
its predisposition,
the way the dahlia determines space
long before its pompous bloom.

Stand on former ground
before the pull of underpinnings,
before the fingered
cracks of stone.

Bend low
to the caterpillar's dream
of flight. Tell it
to wait.

Find the pause
between the song of old and new
where the lyric crossed
its arms and leaned back.

Think of feather-loping on the wind
when air was lighter than a puff
and dust was only
an intention.

# Song for the Hours

O railroad spike—rusting in the field next to the splintered tracks I walked
  one summer alone into my father's past—I held you hot from the sun,
  heavy in my hand.
O train whistle of woe coming sure as nightfall to someone's porch.
Opossum—cold by the roadside—your babies cling so tight to your nipples
  that the officer has to tug them loose before wrapping them
  into her handkerchief.
O mourning stars, have you lost your appointed place in the heavens?

~~~

O, Donne. Say it again: *Any man's death diminishes me.*
O, Mary Mallon, dubbed Typhoid Mary—poor immigrant no one would miss—
  the creepy kudzu cannot smother the facts of your forced quarantine
  on North Brother Island.
O islands of respite and desolation.
  Pandemic islands. Hart Island.
  Islands choking on rough pavement.
  Islands of justice shot through with holes.
O, Abraham. Say it again: *Here I am.*

~~~

And here am I.
  Walking daily rounds in my courtyard,
  thinking of prisoners at recess tossing balls, jogging, puffing cigs.
I pull weeds, inspect flowers, search for tender leaves, any rosebud;
  pause in sunlight to watch bumble bees suckle purple blossoms.
I think of those Alcatraz inmates who lovingly designed and landscaped gardens
  on that island.
St. Francis of Assisi, in moments of loneliness and exile, withdrew to caves.

~~~

This morning's breeze tastes like freedom.
The azure-colored wind spinner next to the iron swing
goes wild, turning and turning.
I was once a child sitting on the city bus next to my mother,
holding a windmill out the window.
Joy coursed through my being,
mingled with fumes from the streets.

Sweetness of bird song returns.
O wind chimes of my hours.

I am here.

# A Jar of Rain

Wrapped in threadbare & faded
cotton towels, snuggled
between the hub & Beth Ann's
sneakered feet, the faint
sloshing of jarred rainwater
too muffled to hear
above road whine & Rolling
Stones on the tape deck.
But like some rare & fragile
egg, she nestled it
there all four hundred long miles
east to Manhattan.
When her brother left Wheeling,
it had been springtime.
He allowed how he'd miss it—
yearning green mountains,
misty Ohio River,
& mostly the rain,
how it sluiced off mom's rooftop
to collect & brim
in an old metal oil drum,
how when he would thwack
its steel side with his finger,
rings would shiver toward
dark water's chilly center.
He would miss the rain,
& they would miss him,
gone to the city, dream job
among skyscrapers
the "big break" of his young life.
They'd sung the theme from
*The Mary Tyler Moore Show*
together that night
he first heard he'd been hired

& flung cloth napkins
high at the kitchen ceiling,
"You're gonna make it
after all" deflecting off
walls & rising like
hymnal passages till dawn.
Alvin hit a bump.
*Careful*, she hissed, her left leg
swiveling on raised
toes, hard up against the jar.
It was what she could
still do, the only thing more:
to wash what ashes
were left of his—gutter
to river to sea—
with West Virginia rainfall
dipped up from a drum
whose surface October had
started to freeze over.
Mick Jagger was belting out
"Paint It Black." She saw
the brimming hole in a sky-
line she'd never seen
before begin to unfold.

# At the Co-op, with Dependent Clauses

You say you came for peanuts, for onions and a knobby squash, for kale, an early apple. *That knowledge, like spindrift, scatters.* You say you need soup, vitamins, patchouli oil, a 10-lb. bag of rice to lend you heft. *That raven never lies.* You say you need to spoon out an ounce of dill or zatar or cardamom or nutmeg or thyme. *That mind confuses itself with matter.* You say it's cheese you crave, miso's salty kiss, the kick of cider pressed right here in the valley. *That snow releases pain.* You always come with a bag of old bags, with a hunger for bread shaped by hands you know, for the hive of talk around a pot of tea. *That love travels, as does hate, on breath.* Again and again you come here, as if by some call, by some need to feel the slight give of the floorboards beneath your feet. *That stories thicken with age, with rage.* And to know that under those boards is a basement dug into the earth, solid ground for times of great joy, and now of great fear. *That the end nests in the beginning.*

> The sun stays its course, even when we do not, we the people of abundance, merry in rut and glut, cherry-cheeked with glad tidings, bloated with good cheer. The hour of reckoning upon us, our past is unmasked, our penance, *that all violence is domestic.*

## Sovereignty

Can be fragile, easy
to fade or be erased, all

It takes is a single heavy hand,
a legend thrown

Like a gauntlet, the hand that opens
a country's body, an autopsy.

Nothing says empire
like a flag, says republic like fabric

Stretched & strung, swathes
of land tethered, a sanguine stitch

Of the tongue,    language conquers
from within      before the blade

Separates flesh and kin,
breath & the line, all

Broken by a wall
& a people's history

Crumbling in another's wake

# It Strikes a Contemporary

Like a voice from beyond the pale,
he sends me another email.
Twenty years of what he clearly
sees he wants to make clear to me.
It began with the hijacked planes:
"Who owned them?" "Who was the brains?"
"Who managed to leave the Towers?"
as if he or I had some power,
some visionary cast of eye,
that could ferret truth from lie.
"You know this internet," he stung
me with blame and blessing, wishing
my research would validate
what odd facts he had learned of late.
He rehashed worries: Those others
are the source of all our bothers;
that old time John Birch party line
became increasingly inane.
"Billionaire Jewish lasers in space!!!"
If I could I'd laugh in his face.
He sent selfies dressed in camo
wearing belt on belt of ammo.
He no longer needed my slant.
I was replaced and supplanted
by sources he was sure were good.
He wanted to save me if he could,
extend the old brotherly hand,
a man helping his fellow man.
"WE'RE BEING ATTACKED!!!" his email yelled.
"We've begun to attack ourselves,"
I replied feeling confident
those would be the last notes we sent.

# Myopia, Fall, 2001

Because you can't see
how your house needs cleaning,
you can walk guilt-free into the fall.
It's September, after all:

first wind in a month
lifts leaves, their undersides tinged red.
Your shadow's a stranger—
so quick, so fresh, after August's long burn—

and, though you can't see
the sharp markings of a jay,
you know that cheeky blue streak
for what it is.

Through Martino's tinted window
a familiar shape touches the wrist
of a dark-haired woman.
He might not really be your husband.

Your heart tolls a warning
but you don't look closer, you
hurry home to be comforted
by what you know is yours—

your grandmother's rocking chair,
these family photos,
the gray cat half-opening
her green, predatory eyes.

On the radio you hear terror
crashed through this clear sky,
their voices all stutter and blur.
Though you live 1,000 miles

from New York, you must
get your sons out of school. Now.
You pick up the phone.
Your mind fogs over,

lifts from your body,
sees your hand as a foreign object.
You breathe it in, odorless and colorless,
this particular air of the new century.

# I Was to be Tested for Cancer that Morning

On the radio the NPR report said
a plane crashed into the World Trade Center.

It would be the first plane.
None of that whole day made it to color:

the ultrasound, the cat scan, the news,
which only came in sound,

which the silent gathering
doctors and nurses in the hallway switched off

when they saw me. In 9 days, I would be 11.

When the flight number came out, I tried
to use it as an omen for my body.

Benign? Malignant? I counted 9-1-1 on my knuckles.

~~~

A notion from childhood: emergencies
manifest in the body and the world

at once. *Synesthesia,*
translated from the Greek,

means "to perceive together":
This shortness of breath. These muscle aches.

This white supremacist insurrection.
These half a million dead Americans.

This second mass
found in my body shortly before the pandemic.

The crushed towers. The crowned virus.
The smashing of the Capital doors.

These fevers. These sore throats. This loss of taste.

## After Zazen

Three boys in England
     swallowed stones,
he said, and had to have their stomachs
       cut and sewn.
Not pumped? I didn't ask. So heavy,
      stones.
They must be fetched, even when they've been thrown
down throats that young and small.
        *You can't blame them.*
*They want so much to die.* And no one asked
anything more. We didn't want
     to know them,
the boys who made heaviness
     manifest.


That morning our country
     had invaded
another country.
    We felt bereft.
Ashamed. The Buddhist priest finished
his story. We saw how suffering
     woke
to find itself alive again,
    famished.

# Lament

The Dipper above the house
looks dry tonight, lovers
traveling along its handle for thousands of years.

There is the white around the robin's eye
and some reason why, some religion why.
Young clouds seen drinking from the sea

perish without a soul
while the flag of a grateful nation
is folded and placed in a zip-lock bag.

Left behind, the strict utility of things.
The garage, the door to the garage,
the teeth of the saw.

There is the dusky pink
along the dark shoulders
of an heirloom tomato

and the old mother
seated in her garden chair,
no one left to show the world to.

## Safety Nets

**September 11, 2001**

My son tells me the sky is
Heavy with clouds of angry black smoke.

*There was a man, a broken window*
*I saw him jump.*

He taps a pencil on his worksheet,
His spelling words offer no answers.

*I saw him float, arms twisting*
*past a hundred floors.*
*The teacher kept the sound off.*

I chop the salad. Stir the soup. Listen.
I touch the hollow cave of my throat
Expecting to find a lump,
Something to say.

*Did someone catch him?*

I watch the worry of the falling man
Cut deep into my son's soft face.
I reach out and take his untouched homework.
Fold it and slide it into his backpack.
Tuck it away.

There will be more important tests,
People he may one day need to catch.
Safety nets.

## January 6, 2021

Words of hate
The sky fouled with rage and lies
Push forward over flimsy barriers.
Windows are broken.

Once again, my son is called upon
to bear witness to the falling man.
Tears blind my eyes
Will he know what to do?

Like a shadow from another day
I see his daughter,
Trapped at school.
I am too far away to catch her.
I call, but before I can speak
He answers,
*I have her, we are on our way home.*
*She's safe.*

# Blossom

What is a wound but a flower
dying on its descent to the earth,
bag of scent filled with war, forest,
torches, some trouble that befell
now over and done. A wound is a fire
sinking into itself. The tinder
serves only so long, the log holds on
and still it gives up, collapses
into its bed of ashes and sand. I burned
my hand cooking over a low flame,
that flame now alive under my skin,
the smell not unpleasant, the wound
beautiful as a full-blown peony.
Say goodbye to disaster. Shake hands
with the unknown, what becomes
of us once we've been torn apart
and returned to our future, naked
and small, sewn back together
scar by scar.

# Nachtmusik

Like him, she is old. Her neck curves like the violin's,
whose long harsh kiss shows on her jaw when she turns
to the tuning fork she's spanked on her knee,
her pursed lips drawing in the long thin A.

"Beethoven tonight? Mozart, Haydn? Brahms?"
she gloats absently over the sheets to his usual shrug:
he goes back to touching the cello strings with his thumbs.
She lifts her bow, and its hair falls loose from the frog

like a girl's. "Ach. It's always something, isn't it?
How we play such fragile things, I don't know,
they could fall apart in our hands." With her second bow
she tunes again. He doesn't see her rosin it;

bent over the cello's shoulder he has the sense
of remembering Berlin, the night a bomb
buried the bridegroom and all but one of his friends,
the night he knelt outside his gaping home

and heard the grand piano fall five floors—
heard its last five monstrous chords
that blotted out for years all the Bach he knew.
"Mozart, then," he says, and so they play.

# Tuesday

It's Tuesday, 9/11, and special
pastries for Peggy's birthday
surprise at the office.

Little Peter wanders around,
looks for his school backpack.
Cold lunches lay on the kitchen counter.
Baby Lily needs teething gel
& I need four more arms & two hours.

Husband Dave packs his lunch,
grabs briefcase and scurries
to catch the subway into the city.
I juggle, wrangle up kids and collect
bags like a circus clown.

Today, gray ash clouds haze overhead,
like a blanket of fog. Dark smoke
billows in the distance like a volcano.

More sirens and fire engines blare.
It's the apocalypse, or the End Rapture
Mom warned me about.

## Fort Bragg

When the snow falls, all of post
shuts down like no war is
going on. Perhaps the higher-ups
decide to let those left behind,
for the moment, savor the chance
to shape snowmen with their children
or lie beside another warm body.
Probably it is lack of preparedness.
What happens after: the snow melts,
permeates fractures in asphalt on
Normandy, Ardennes, Bastogne,
European places famous for dead men,
now used as street names where,
for the time being, no soldiers
will be training. The snow sits
as water, freezes in frigid air
into ice. What happens is the
molecules expand, opening their
arms like the universe, like all of us
reaching out for someone to arrive,
until the black asphalt breaks, and
the soldiers of our hearts go
back to work, cleaning up the wreckage.

## Letter to Bill Heyen

I never said thanks for the invitation
to write something, but nothing
would come, nothing but the paralyzing image
of that office worker in mid-air, a man,
his necktie pointing up

toward the window he leaped from.
I was a hostage to moods: anger and sadness,
the typical swings. Mostly I was numb, sometimes
even envious of faces twisted and crying on television news.
Almost four months later, I'm in Sun Devil Stadium.

Not quite wanting to be, I'm at the Fiesta Bowl
with a family of in-laws and friends—
all hard-core fans but me. I'm beginning to seethe,
thinking about football—the tail that wags a university,
the academic slack that's cut for jocks,

the cynical coaches, the scholar-athlete charade,
the whole sleazy business
that grows in sync with our addiction to sports.
Anyway, I'm sitting there with this new-found anger,
feeling like Malvolio among the happy fans,

their faces painted with bison and ducks.
But I'm nervous too
because it's that same kind of perfect day,
sunny and blue, and passenger jets are low overhead
on their last leg into Sky Harbor just west of us.

I try to focus on pre-game pass drills and warm ups
when six Air Force skydivers exit
a DeHavilland prop from ten thousand feet,
their canopies yellow, green, and white.
With binocs I watch them tack and spiral in.

Each one tries for the red rectangle at mid-field.
The last diver trails a big rippling flag,
the Stars and Stripes,
and nails the target. My breath catches,
everything blurs. I'm choking back sobs,

eyes wet behind sunglasses I'm glad to be wearing
when an Apache gunship roars over the stadium,
and my right arm lifts on its own, my hand in a fist.
I whisper *Yes*. I can barely believe it.
But others too, sniffling, handkerchiefs out.

A Mexican guy with a moustache, his cheeks
shiny with tears. The woman next to me,
touching Kleenex to her face, takes my arm.
Suddenly, after months, I'm at the sorrow of Ground Zero
with a deep sense of the team I belong to.

Valéry was right: we're locked outside ourselves.
Which is why poems exist. Something in me
wanted out, I found the right key, and it finally emerged,
but late, Bill, too late for the book. Sorry I couldn't deliver.

# The Day Everything Changed

I remember when word came on the morning radio:
a plane had crashed into one of the Twin Towers.

I was driving to work on backroads and so pictured
some errant bi-plane's nose bumping into a steel wall

and falling to the ground, pesky mosquito.
But a commercial jet had pierced the building,

probably a terrorist attack, and another plane
was arrowing toward the second tower. Almost

impossible, but that plane hit its target, then
the first tower collapsed. Removed from screens,

sans cellphone, I'd still not seen a single image.
But I saw the second tower go down, surrounded

by colleagues in the teachers lounge. You know
the rest: a trauma loop of men and women

jumping out of open windows, clouds of rubble,
people fleeing, ash covered. Hard to believe now

but I made my way to the classroom and waited
for my students to show. And many of them did.

We sat there for an hour or more, allowing
one another to cry and yell and wonder aloud

what our world would be like now, and how
we might never fit ourselves into its new narrative.

# Early Morning, Downtown 1 Train

In this car packed with closed faces, this tube
    of light tunneling through darkness: two sleeping boys, so close
        I could touch them without reaching—their smooth brown faces,

planed cheekbones like Peruvian steppes leading from
    or to some beautiful ruin. Boys so alike they must be brothers.
        And the small, worried man they sprawl against, too young to seem

so old: father. How far have they come? How far to go?
    They sleep as only loved children sleep, wholly, no need
        to tighten or clutch, to fold themselves in. Their heads are thrown back,

mouths open—no, agape, which looks like *agape*,
    the highest form of love, some minister told me long ago.
        As if love is a cupboard of lower and higher shelves, and why bother

reaching if you have hands like the hands of this young father,
    cracked and blistered, stamped with the pattern of shovel or pick.
        For someone must do our digging, and rise in the dark to dress

the children carefully, as these boys are dressed, and pack their knapsacks,
    and ease out of the seat without waking the open-mouthed
        younger one nor the older whose head now rests fully

on the emptied seat . . . but, "My, God," I think
    as the brakes squeal and the father moves quickly to face the door, "he is leaving
        these children, a father leaving his children." The train slows at 50th

and he presses his body against the door, lifting his arms
    above his head—a signal? surrender?—as the door slides open
        and a woman steps in, small and dark like the father, her body

lost in a white uniform. She touches his sleeve, something
          passes between their eyes. Not sadness exactly, but ragged
               exhaustion, frayed edges meeting: his night her day, her night

his day, goodbye hello. She slides onto the seat, lifting
          one son's head to her lap. His mouth is still open, his body limp.
               She smoothes his collar.  Her small hands move to his lips,

closing them gently the way one closes the mouth
          of the recently dead. But the boy is not dead. Just sleeping,
               an arm thrown over his brother. His mother near.

# STOP

*March 21, 2003,*
  *the second day of the War on Iraq*

Spring finally pedaled past
on her beat-up bike with rusty fenders,
singing pensive wordless songs
that filled just-opened doors and windows,

wearing a blue-sky sundress
and chartreuse helmet from which a braid
dangled thickly down her back
that stayed perfectly straight as she rode,

level arms stretched out sideways
like an acrobat balancing on the high wire,
long bare pale legs steadily
propelling her toward the bloody sign

and its imperative refrain,
ignored on the road we're headed down again.

## One Morning in America

Sara sets the mug in the sink,
but carefully, fingertips brushing
lopsided hearts Ariel painted.
In two hours her fingers are dust.

Carlos sees Cheerios on Miguel's cheek,
tousles his hair, remembers
yesterday he said *Daddy*.
In two hours his great heart bursts.

The breaking of bodies
*Ashes to ashes*

Rescuers look for Sara, for Carlos,
over two thousand more gone
into mist we cannot see
but they look, and listen for breath
even phantom breath,
and they breathe in dust,
become asbestos filters
that no longer work,
cannot process more fire
or shell fire in heated lands we fill
with long, young lines, boys
who once cried *Daddy*,
never enough shaved head soldiers,
flames turn, singe our streets
where we never learned
there weren't enough boys
to fill the rice fields of Asia.

## Let Us Draw Near

*No day shall erase you from the memory of time.*
—Virgil, *The Aeneid*, National September 11 Memorial Museum

Ten days after 9/11 my father's heart exploded, his life collapsing in a matter of moments. We could not find each other in our own familiar streets. We could not ask now how to meet him in the ash. Old-school Catholics, we prayed, "*Adiemus. Adiemus.*"

There were two of me, one loving, one late in loving. I set aside the national mourning, which I could not withstand. When you said he can rest now, asked how you could help, that brought no calm, and no peace came when you recalled your own lost ones.

No new perspective came when the news returned again, again to the three thousand gone, to acts of heroism, to horrors visited upon survivors, to tender personal interviews news cycle after news cycle that I took in while ignoring, ignoring the entire wrecked nation.

Today my sister, youngest of the five children, has died before her turn. She has ended her participation in our grim middle-age sibling tag game of electronic messaging, burning each other with teasing grief, our way to touch but not be done with familial anniversaries of mistaking one obliterated story for another.

How many further words are farther out of reach. How few near are terribly nearer. The expression of tribute the nation leaves for the nation is Virgil's martial words, as out of context as severed heads in snow. No monuments stand long, and in that I find consoling bitter satisfaction.

Ten days after your deaths (and only incidentally your lives) were lovingly commemorated, I did, I did turn off the tube, unplugged you three-thousand dead from my living memory.

The two of me, one loving and one late in loving, called to mind their names, words towering over all other inscriptions. Hers was Wendy, meant to echo his. Wendell.

## Winter Hard

When the forest caught fire, the horses
obeyed a fear greater
than what had been bred into them,
broke down the stable, and stampeded
for the opening in the trees,
which was the lake, which was water.

Of course they headed towards
the alternative, liquid,
unlike the material that made
or was burning up the hard world
they had to escape.

It was the bombardment
of Central Forces that started the fire,
in Finland. This is Malaparte's story.

By his account, hundreds of horses
sped through flames, splashed in,
and, the second they entered, the lake
froze solid.

Which makes no sense. But never mind
science. The idea stays with us.

Snap—they were suspended,
coated and sealed, suddenly. And singly,
though the herd had entered as a whole.

It could be called tragic because
they were entombed, heads up,
so all winter, soldiers could see
the last shapes failed struggles take.

It could be asserted that the animal face—
flared nostrils, flung mane,
all frozen—is a simplified expression
of human experience.

Something might be said about that war,
what we fight now.

But to merit retelling
there need not be double meaning.
It's hard enough that a horse
had to seek escape and was denied it,
even in decay.

Divisions are hard, how one side does not
see itself in the other, or crystallized,
cast in that clear ice.

The horror of each is its own,
alone. Beyond comparison,

and compassion. The soldiers are said
to have walked among the horses
like a sculpture garden on their smoke breaks.
Casually, to be by themselves,
between the bodies, they went
to light their little fires.

The individual man's flame was too small
to make anything melt.
And not even summer could turn
the sharp edge of this back to water.

## To Die

for a student lost in the Towers

He went away to be a banker, a man of economics,
but first had to pass my class of children's books.
Alice his favorite, Pan next, their defiance
his kind of bare-faced sass.
When I saw the first tower go,
then its twin, I thought of him
laughing, scratching notes on this page.
I'd bet all my money he went down
the rabbit hole in a good-hearted rage,
defying every injury, promising himself
this adventure was an awfully awfully
big and endless dream.

## 8:46 AM

Stopping by the PO, I find
my words come back, poems
in the SASE postmarked Chicago.
By 8:46 it does not matter
though I do not know that
in the capsule of a classroom,
teaching Hemingway's war to students
who do not remember Viet Nam.
All of us smug, remote from atrocities.
*We are not in a war now*, I say smiling,
more words to come back.

At break with colleagues
I learn of words lost: incomplete
conversations in air
and buildings, blown up
between noun and verb,
one syllable and the next,
snippets of final vowels,
consonants left in hallways,
by the water cooler,
on the stairs—
all potential words.

# In Retrospect: 9/11

Praise the firefighters who went thundering
up the stairs that September morning,
and weighted down:
uniforms, hats, boots, oxygen tanks, fire hoses.
Praise the long red trucks with ladders
raising silver into smoke and dust
from the boom of concrete and metal
that scorched the asphalt face of earth.
Praise the water's arc that rose,
a drizzling tongue that could not lick
its way to the tall burning floors
when the windows blew out
when the walls cracked and burst
when the floors collapsed
when the firefighters would not abandon
workers scrambled in ash.
Praise the firefighters who went thundering in.

## A Sickness in the Air

September 10, 2001, I flew down to the city for an interview and
meeting with my publisher. There seemed to be a sickness in the air
that day no one explained, a dread and menace among the noise and
smells and frantic rush. Returning to La Guardia that afternoon I found
my plane held on the ground for hours, as storm followed storm, until
the crew were canceling the flight for good, when suddenly the all
clear came, to get us home long after midnight. Next day I watched
the city freeze, as people dripped from the towers like condensation,
above the fires and manes of toxic ash, and steel beams fell on those
below—beginning this new age of wars, two wars abroad that never
end, and one at home to rip the fabric of our nation apart, these
twenty years, and counting . . .

# Up North

The Cessna in my head transformed
into an airliner. Bloomberg TV brought
digital images via the Internet
and we watched them seagull-like
plunge into our homes.

Typical New Yorkers, business as usual,
we tried to focus but our loved ones,
What about our loved ones?

Get our daughter out of school, I said.
Why are you still at work? Get out of there! Go!
Go to your mothers! she said, in not so gentle tones.

Wrestling with fear I switched to grunt mode
figuring eight years of Marine Corps'
repetitious training would finally pay off.
Around me, frozen emotions.

Get out of there! echoed in my head,
and I left, stopping only at the lobby to beg
my co-worker one last time,
"Come with me to the Bronx." She stayed.

I marched not thinking about the miles that lie ahead.
Just focusing on the line of us walking north.
Our New York gait was a little different that morning,
the sense of purpose that distinguishes the natives
from the tourist wasn't firm.
The surrealism of the moment
made our movements uncommitted.

We entered Central Park mathematically calculating
how far the skyscrapers along the edge
would protrude into the park
if they too would have toppled.

Up the path we moved, good Samaritans
we never stop being. On our route,
defeated by the moment on top of rocks, people cried,
in disbelief they embraced and the sound we heard
was a whisper in our hearts. We knew
we felt the same.

And we marched on through Harlem
a world apart. Tired in so many ways
a gypsy cab running shuttles from the park
to the edge of the water, I rode
until traffic allowed us no further
and I marched again, up north.

Across the bridge into the Bronx,
rode the BX1, passed the old neighborhood.
On the Grand Concourse I struggled to glance
out of the crowded bus and thanked God
Yankee Stadium was unharmed.

Soon after I arrived at my mother's apartment,
a place, a neighborhood I knew so well.
Yet shaken, I was safe among the family photos
and familiar faces, Up North.

# The Knife, Now

You might be Abraham
trudging up that slope

or equally Isaac—

you can't tell by how your
feet fall on the path

or the color of the sky.

Maybe you're
the ram at his daily browse

ensnared by the bush,

or the angel summoned
out of itself mid-hover—

no end to it

to the burning
on top of the mountain

to the bared throats.

We try to take in something we
can't quite compass

each of us looking

up

## War, a Word

*No Germanic nation in earliest historic times had a word meaning*
*"war." Romance-speaking peoples found no nearer equivalent than*
*"werra,"—v. to bring into confusion or discord.*
                    *—Chambers Dictionary of Etymology*

1121 CE - v. of action
Before its name
it was
a human enterprise
spinning words
toward dictionaries

*war crime, war dance, warfare,*
*war paint, warship, war horse,*
*warpath, warplane, war zone*

1991–*n.* of confused pride:
"Didja see how we kicked
some major ass in the Gulf?"

9/11/2001–*n.* of conflict
from *werra,*
root also for *worst*
*adj.* of superlative degree
flashing in sunlight.

A woman knocks
on a neighbor's door
with a basket of tomatoes
from the garden.
A team hurls
bowling balls down the alley,
pins crashing.

A father holds a photo high,
a firefighter digs in debris.

Floating from the ashes,
*war*, from *werra*
settles,
comfortable on the President's lips.

In a Manhattan bookstore
outdated post cards revolve on a rack,
New York City's skyline spinning.

## Television, Trees

In my lap you doze, your breathing
shortened, slowly drifting deeper.

Will it snow? you seem to ask,
if words are also what a lover's body asks.

On TV the planes explode,
too tinny in our tiny speaker;

out the window, woods and clouds,
the sky thinning, full.

Darling, what's that noise?
You grimace, rub your nose.

Such pageantry in cruelty,
while the snow begins unbidden.

~~~

Can smoke be hard?
The birch tree peels in curls

that look like smoke but aren't;
the bare soul consoles itself,

wrapped in facts, in fat.
Maybe every tree is

cloaked in smoke, expectant—
and maybe when I die I will become

what I have always been,
empty in the world.

~~~

A crow defines a bare elm,
the wind serrated.

Is heaven a place to come or go?
Heaven is smooth, says the snow.

Heaven is cold.
Beyond the meadow two birches

lean like lovers
propped up by each other.

In a different season they might seem
less festive, gaudy, gift-wrapped.

~~~

Hi, Mom, a soldier waves.
Snow shoulders every tree,

catches in the crotches, stays.
In my lap, my lover grumbles dreamfully,

a furnace kicking on unseen.
Tonight the news ends with the wind

rattling the upstairs, rising,
whistling, acute.

Bye, Mom. Don't be sad.
It's only television that we're on—

and the wind and the snow
are ours to sleep through,

the birches bending to an X,
fingers crossed, a promise.

# Transport

Photograph of a woman in Berlin
after a bombing raid, 1942

Half human, half monster, wearing
    a gas mask, pushing a baby carriage
hurriedly past a movie marquee

where part of a word—L O R I A
    is visible through smoke.  She's like
the figure from the movie *The Fly*

that I saw in Berlin when I was eleven,
    an army brat afraid of getting lost,
but lonely enough to go out.

A scientist experiments with a transport machine,
    and decides to enter it himself,
not knowing a fly has flown in.  The man

emerges with the arm and head of a fly,
    and the fly has escaped
with a small human head and arm.

The fly must be found.  The white carriage
    is rolling along, the baby inside
 might have its own mask made

like a body suit, but air needs pumping in.
    Hurry, hurry.  An infant longing
for its mother's face, a mother

playing peek-a-boo, disappearing
    only briefly then returning
with a smile.  The wife tells her son

to try and catch the white fly
    he's seen, and screams
when she finds the maid with a swatter.

Hadn't she told her husband how frightened
    she was: *Electronics, rockets, earth satellites,*
*supersonic flight, everything going so fast.* All

his reassurance that life as we know it
    will change, and humanity will never fear again.
The huge black head of the husband

when the wife pulled the cover off wasn't as scary
    as the close-up of the fly, its human face
and fat tongue shrieking, *Help me, Help me.*

## Fallen Gardens

April leaves its glory to the warmth
and whims of May, another dry summer
in the forecast. Doesn't the end of any month
ache to return to beginnings—tender

green opening to white, white to green,
even though the stunning fullness
of a branch bent with pale blossoms
is never enough to bring back a son.

No breeze can gentle the knowledge
that somewhere in old Babylon
a father pleads for Allah, for any god
to grant him Abraham's deliverance.

Bereft of angels, his sky instead
carries a stinging wind circling the man
forced by soldiers to lower a gun
to the crown of his son's head,

a young informer broken
to the ground at his father's feet,
his forehead pressed in dust
that will rise and cover everyone.

# Jim

1.

I walked New York's dirty streets all day with a 35mm camera in my hand, heat rising from creosote subways, taking pictures of buildings. Their taut geometry, their parallel lines rising into the sky, led me to a metal door that opened onto the roof of the World Trade Center. It was 1975, a year after high-wire artist Philippe Petit stepped off and walked to the other tower. The view this day wasn't so hot, just a stiff wind and a skyline that seemed removed from the rest of Manhattan, unguarded, alone. Twenty-five years later, my brother Jim would have an office there.

2.

Nobody told a joke better than Jim. We lived in the City at the same time, swapping intel on oddball restaurants, street fairs and art shows. He took me to see Koyaanisqatsi, "life out of balance," an auteur film that took a hammer to skyscrapers and other embodiments of our mad world. Clouds casting shadows on natural vistas contrasted with crowds sleepwalking in Times Square conformity. Escalators at the World Trade Center were filmed in accelerated furious motion upward, as the kinetic neon of cars traced lines below. A rocket headed skyward exploded, spinning to earth in flames.

3.

Jim was upstate with his wife on Labor Day weekend, visiting our folks and kayaking on Cayuga Lake for the first time. A week later he was back in his office in the North Tower, hanging in after a downsizing for his stocks to bounce back on his way to an early retirement. I'd left the city long ago and was standing in my Southern yard, a cup of coffee in hand, when the first plane hit. They never did find his body.

4.

A piece of bone got picked off the sorter at Fresh Kills landfill where they took the Tower debris—which is why I was at the New York Medical Examiner's office, its pale municipal green walls like every classroom, cop show or city hall on TV. I heard her high heels echoing off the walls as she approached. Blunt force trauma, she said, explaining how my brother got small enough to fit in a test tube. I went out a side door and got blasted by smoke off a barbecue grill, hot dogs and sausages simmering in flames for guys still on the pile.

5.

Hibakusha, A-bomb elders from Japan, came to New York to see another Ground Zero. When Hiroshima and Nagasaki vanished, they remained, by coincidence or miracle, to bear witness forever after with their wounded lives. You lost two buildings, one of them said. We lost two cities. I lost the world. I lost my brother.

6.

St. Paul's Chapel, tiny sanctuary in the shadow of the Towers, survived the maelstrom of the collapse and played host to the rescue crews. The following spring I was in its backyard cemetery and heard birds in the trees. When scraps of paper ticker-taped down, they built nests.

7.

A flatbed truck bowed under the weight of a New York Fire Department bell at the 9/11 commemoration: Ring a bell for the person you lost, they said. I put down my newspapers, felt for the heavy clapper below and gave it a swing. The big sound swelled and went off among the buildings, returning empty-handed.

## Loss Calls the Cops

He's done this before.
Calls the cops
to say his best friend
went fishing and won't answer
his phone. Loss stands on the bank,
brow furrowed, watching the divers
and inhaling the smell
of the muck the wrecker pulls up.
There's never anybody there.
It's just that feeling he gets
sometimes, that bloated feeling,
chains dragging his chest.

# Beneath September

September 11, 2016

On CNN, the reporter interviews a priest
from Manhattan, asks him what long-term effect
9/11 has had on us all. The priest says,
*For fifteen years we've all been walking around*
*with a lump in our throats.*

I was an ocean away,
in Ireland, already afternoon,
in the stands of the Galway Races.
The boys we were meeting had just
heard the news on a taxi's radio.

Inside, people placing their bets
at each glass window. All the TV screens
that tracked the race flickered off
and the news came on, and we had
bought Guinnesses,

and we held them, half full, unaware
they were in our hands as the second plane hit—
or a replay of the second plane hitting,
again and again.  I was in Ireland,
in the country four of my great grandparents,

Honora and John, Esther and Samuel,
had left for Ellis Island.
Ten days earlier, my parents
had driven me through New York City
to the Newark Airport.

From the backseat as we crossed
the George Washington Bridge,
the Towers. Ten days later,
Flight 93 would also take off from Newark.

This was the last place I would see

my father alive, who would die
in his sleep that November.
There he stood, bottom of the escalator,
in a light green polo shirt, khaki shorts,
boat shoes and white socks pulled

halfway up his shins, waving.
I no longer remember where he said he was
when the planes hit—perhaps in a van
delivering flowers, his new
retirement job. We will keep asking

each year *where were you?*
until no one was anywhere,
until a new world grows up,
pushes up beneath September.
My mother, up late one night

watching the news—Ground Zero,
family members still there, xeroxed copies
of the missing gripped in their hands.
My mother, falling asleep to this,
asked God if there's anything she can do

to relieve their suffering—
to let it be done.
The next morning she found my father,
cold, unmoving in the bed.
I flew home for his funeral,

leaving Ireland before the semester ended,
before a planned trip to Amsterdam,

my plane ticket exchanged for a flight
back to Newark. The embers
of the Towers still smoldering

though I didn't look out the window.
Several of my aunts and uncles, my sister
met me there. In a rented limo,
we rode back to our old white house
in Connecticut, rode through

a tangle of thru-ways, potholes,
we rode home through the flags.
In my memory they were everywhere—
draped from every possible bridge,
and homemade USA banners and posters,

some in tatters. I craned my neck,
the flags hung from the balconies
of the steep apartments.
Uncle John, sitting across from me,
noticed my noticing, lifted his hands,

palms open to the gray canyons, said
*It's been incredible—*
*you've missed it all.*

## Planting the Garden

Last fall, four boys stood
on the back porch like snipers,
steadied b.b. guns on the rail,
and fired at G.I. Joes propped on fence posts.
Now body parts of dead soldiers
lie fallow in dirt like volunteer radishes
and I don't know what I am raising.
These are boys whose skin is smooth as young squash.
War is only what they read about
under covers when the house is still,
dying young is plastic soldiers
gasping in the bean rows.
I pause, my hoe a makeshift crutch,
and cradle a toy face in my hand.
I touch the brown eyes,
the perfect part of hair,
straight as fence wire, just right of the middle.
So like my son's.
I lay him down,
tuck him in soil.

# Twenty Years Beyond

Who would have thought

planes flying into skyscrapers,
people throwing their bodies earthward,
firefighters poisoning themselves
to rescue the desperate

was not an extreme end
but the beginning.

A giant breaking
in the new world order.

A shifting from construction
to mulish destruction.

Only now the wreckage
is not perpetrated
by jihadis

but by ourselves
against ourselves,

a civil war
of attack and denial,
lies and avoidance

not seen
in over a century.

Such missiles we hurl at
each other, such flagpoles,
armored shields, microphones,
social media posts
as weapons of our rage.

Who can survive such
bombardment?

And who can
assemble the ruins

that like eyes
roam amid rubble

and stare back

against a broken sky?

## Infamous Days

It was one of those days when you remember
exactly where you were,
like my father remembered leaving
Grauman's Chinese Theater
December 7, '41, hearing
about Pearl Harbor.
Or the day I found my mother wringing
her hands, sobbing in fear,
the day that Kennedy was shot.

Images of the Twin Towers
destroyed in suicidal hatred
are seared into our brains like
a broken newsreel we watch again
and again, wishing the images away,
doomed to remember forever the victims
running for their lives trying to flee
the fire and smoke and debris
of that post-modern Vesuvius.

New York, the place and stuff
of dreams. A place where a girl child
skipped down Fifth Avenue, delighted
in the Bronx Zoo, fell asleep to the crooning
of a singing cowboy at Madison
Square Garden; these memories now
overshadowed by that infamous day when
we lost the last of our innocence.

Infamous days come almost daily now
with bombings, school shootings, mass
murder, crowding our calendar like
a cursed dance card filled
with malevolent suitors.
Infamous days fueling
a pandemic of hate adding 1/6
to 9/11, turning us against those deemed
the other, until there is no one left to hate
but ourselves.

# Witness the Whole World

As fractured eggshell of a woman,
I carry the long litany of the lost
with me everywhere I go.
I pocket the tragedy,
fly to London anyway.
There for a poetry tour,
I do not remember any of the poems,
but I remember a woman, a black Brit
who made tea for a few of us in her flat
after the gig. I remember her mahogany hands,
how she made a ritual of making tea.
How her hands danced in circles
as she cut and squeezed the lemon.
I remember how each gesture soothed me like prayer.
I watched as she added sugar and a little cream.
Then, she gently stirred the cup of tea
—handed it to me. I sat and sipped.
How I wanted to weep from this kindness.

I remember one night at 2 a.m.
and an African man ranting at the TV
high up in a corner of the convenience store,
"Good. I am happy that happened to America,
 America has been bombing—
terrorizing my country for years."
I did not know which country he was from.
I only remember being burnt by his rage,
and feeling the truth in his fire.
I remembered my own country
and our motto: *We will never forget.*
And it is true. I will never forget,
but I keep on remembering
all the sorrows everywhere.

# US

The professor pulls
the screen down,
and projects a map
of the world onto it.

*As you all know,*
*we have been at war*
*in several countries*
*for many years now.*
*Not to embarrass anyone,*
*but can anyone point*
*to those countries*
*on the map?*

No one can.
*OK*, the professor says, *OK.*
And then—

*Well, here's the thing—*
*most of those who*
*we're at war with,*
*when asked to point*
*to* US, *can.*

# I Will Meet You There

*I looked on the earth, and lo, it was waste and void;*
*and to the heavens, and they had no light.*
                                        *—Jeremiah 4*

There was a woman sitting in a coffee shop.
It was morning. She was with her latté.
She looked out the window, mostly street,
everything in motion in every direction.

She came back to her coffee, whose wisp
of steam issued from a small oval hole
in the plastic lid. Her brother was ascending
the elevator elsewhere.  Emails awaited him,

and blue sky, which was not in view either there
or at the coffee shop, which nobody noticed anyway,
because it sailed to the end of summer. She tired
already, thinking of her concluding chores,

among which was their mother, whose swelling
complaints they would prefer to avoid, but joined
to manage. And of the emails? One said,
"I will meet you there in the afternoon."

The distance was one mile. They had both
measured it once, sitting before a map,
like some kind of shared radiant thought.
There were coordinates, the kind siblings

shared like a supernatural gift, though no one
believed in such things. The sky was unchanged.
The wind pushed under the park trees, as you
would raise an elderly woman to take her pills.

Elsewhere another wind pushed at treetops
that swayed begrudgingly like the smokestacks
of early ships. No guy-wires fastened them,
and one day they would topple without ceremony.

## American Back Porch

Written for, and read at, the 2002 9/11 memorial
event, conducted at Greensboro College

Was that a shooting star
or a Tomahawk missile
streaking across yon horizon?
It's hard to tell from here.
No report seems forthcoming.
It used to be you lived on the front porch
where everyone could see your business.
Not no more. I'm tucked here,
where my adjustable lawn chair
affords a truncated view of an inscrutable sky
and neighbors whose lives appear in snatches.

I suppose the crickets may carry a coded message
that reveals vital information. If they do,
I'm not privy.

For this impenetrable fortress,
for my daily blessing of ignorance,
where nothing is known
and nothing becomes known,
and nothing shall ever become known,
I am grateful.

# When My Student Tells Me She's Afraid
## to Go to School

we're sitting in the library, tucked
in a corner room. She describes
the week's active shooter scare,

how they all filed outside and waited,
unsure what comes next. Her dark eyes
search mine for reassurance,

something I can't give. Her hair
falls below her shoulders, shiny
as crow's wings folded down her back.

A gunmetal gray sky, heavy
with snow, lurks outside the window
where crocuses bloom. She holds my gaze,

this child of immigrants, high school
junior, an American girl. Her mother
from north Vietnam, father from the South.

Born in North Carolina, she's never left,
but here in this rural mountain town
people still ask, *where are you from?*

She writes poems about her life as *other*,
her plans for college, medical school.
But first she must survive high school.

She fears the classmate with an AK-47
who arrives at school intent on slaughter.
Not that it's happened here—yet.

I want for her what she wants,
safe passage, a path free
of landmines. This sixteen-year-old

never knew a world before
that clear September day
when terrorists shattered everything

we thought we knew about safety.
Even that day when we mourned
together, comforted each other in this

land of immigrants and ignorance,
a boy who looked like her
heard a classmate yell at him, *go back*

*where you came from.* His true answer,
the same as hers—*I am an American.*
But what does that mean? Who gets to tell

her story? She inherited a country
formed from ash and toxic dust, part zombie
apocalypse tale, part Broadway fantasy,

a nation that keeps ending. But she
can begin anew, running toward her fears,
like an airline passenger attacking hijackers.

*You can turn this country toward a new direction.*
*Run, as if your life depends on it.*
Because it does. Because you must.

# For the Moonflower

*And shall not loveliness be loved forever.*
—Euripides

The Tiki torches seethe and sink
like fumes around a Confederate monument.
I turn away from the pole-mounted lamps.
Hold the heat. My eyes widen blink by blink
to put out the night fires in Charlottesville.
A Nazi flag screams in the park.

Smoke loiters nicotine pale
before a coffee cream dawn. Slashed rain
clears the coastal grape air of August.
A cross burning remains the cross
I link to this history. Stand inflamed by it.

Parallel to night fire heat is tear gas.
Riot cops blast its canister at my feet.
The raid stabs chemical into my skin,
lungs, mouth. Its minutiae trembles in my bruises
and scars. The blistering fire has a fog-face,
a blood spilling edge.

When I see the seabirds of Atlantic watersheds
as home, I look to the hills unscorched
by little Hitlers. What's left of the blistering fires
I dump in the trash. Wash off the soot.
This water cleanse ripples with the moonflower.

She never salutes arm raised, palm open, hand down,
a German fuhrer of the Third Reich.

Even as scuffles break out stormed with shouts,
she shows peace, blooms velvety, easy-going.
Post-matinee, no telling how many
comers by starlight ride her lean lapel.
Wink at her melodic but soundless iridescence.

I pull back my hands from the wind scorched,
words scorched over burnt grass.
Silence the last snake on the ground.
I even mourn the brutalities of fire.
Drift and dwindle inside its walls.

The swastika night trickles into a manhole.
When gloom contains me, a caged moth,
the subway train, bus, and car motors
boom a cold manufactured opus in my ears.
Still she leaves in the dust of my DNA little lights
able to spot the cross-burning plots.

I stretch my legs on the bedrock without fire.
The moonflower spirals without smoke
up the trellis, heart-shaped foliage
unfolds her white windward sails
on the wide ship of night.

# Manhood

You were still too little for the new bicycle I'd gotten you, but too big for the tricycle you still liked to ride, and so while the big bike stood unused in the driveway, you rode the tricycle around the cul de sac, knees banging on the handlebars, feet clumsily pedaling, happy to be too big for once for anything, laughing so goofily it made me laugh to see you laugh, which as I watched surprised me the way the plane-less silence in the skies that week surprised us all; 9/11 had just become itself. A new and heady unironic language you couldn't speak without and still be heard had overnight become our lingua franca, an Esperanto we woke up knowing, as if what tumbled down with the towers were the civic Babels of our separate lives, as if we had been blown by the explosions backward to a pre-Babel nearly Edenic understanding, speaking the same tongue inside the same body politic that flexed its outraged muscle through the words we spoke, no matter who we spoke them to. Our good neighbor Rob, the Vietnam Vet, business school professor, church deacon, town council member, wandered over to where I stood. You were shouting watch me daddy watch me, and as you pedaled by he said, "Big boy like you shouldn't ride a girl's bike." The barb of mockery was aimed at me, it seemed, not you. Yet you, not understanding what or why, you got it. Something wasn't right—something I hadn't told you about except perhaps in my too soft understated over-nuanced way, conveyed without explicitly conveying, reluctantly, in stifled anger and impatience, in signals flashing by too quick to notice even while they're felt. You looked at him and then at me, and in the look I saw inchoate bafflement, trace elements of shame, first inklings of an aura of the law that through him, at that moment, had finally found you out. And as you pedaled off, you were just like us now, not smiling, not laughing, serious and dutiful: you too had a job to do, so you did it.

# That Day

### 1. That Day

Metal bones creak and moan
on upper floors. On the phone,
a man says a final good-bye to his wife.

Papers drift and fall
confetti-like from buildings, one body
drops inside death's sudden silence.
We watch the screen, stunned, cannot clear
the images, or lift our frozen eyes or tongues.
We hold one united breath.

What next America?

I take inventory in the Rolodex inside my head—
who do I know that might be dead: old friends,
relatives? My husband on an early morning plane,
United. A jolt in my ears. DC. Dulles.
Two older brothers in the city.
Where are they now? I cannot reach them.

I sit with friends, eyes mesmerized by
repeated visuals, foreign fingers push numbers
into the phone, rings that go unanswered.

### 2. Aftermath

> *There are no X-rays for a person's soul*
> —Brian Jenkins, NPR

If a hijacker will give away his life, his limbs
there is no negotiating, no safe landing possible.

Early on they say airport safety is to blame.
How else could four planes be taken in one day?

What X-ray machine could evaluate a person's good
or bad intentions, or peek inside to see if someone
has a conscience or tainted agenda.

New rules: steak knives removed from first class,
airport cafeterias fill their trays with plastic knives and forks instead.
What about high heels, the spiky ones, earring backings,
granny's knitting needles, travel sewing kits?


### 3. Change

For days the sky goes silent
no take offs or landings, no metal jets trailing smoke lines
across the sky and clouds.
Missing persons and found bodies
replace stock market ticker tapes across the screen.

Flags sprout from every car and house.
I had forgotten how many stripes
there are, how many stars.
At night when I close my eyes
red, white and blue flash
across the darkness.

## That Day

It was a clear day across the vista,
mountain ridges tufted with red oaks
and sugar maples turning a bittersweet orange,
joy in my heart a moment exploding
before I learned ships sank in lower Manhattan,
the fleet of two. On their decks passengers
from different nations traveling together,
screamed for their lives. Some tried to fly
through portholes. That day,
I learned the meaning of the word
machination: a secret scheme of artful design
intended to cause evil, that September day,
joy in my heart gone gray as ash.

# Manhattan Buddha

Straight-backed, seated on the window ledge,
he looks down at traffic pebbling the street
ninety floors below, the hair at the back of his neck
about to catch, nothing but morning air under

his dangled feet. The flames behind him make
the sound of waves trying to clutch the sand
they just can't hold, the way they never could.
He sees it all and smiles. There is no

humbug in him, in his oblique worship
of the horizon, the seagulls, the faithful ferries
dragging like dunked flies across the water;
his face alert as if he watched God watching,

he opens his arms and falls—leaving me here
inside, clinging to myself, the walls on fire.

# DC Suburb, 9/11/2001

after "Jakarta, January" Sarah Kay

By the time a year later when the man
       & the teenage boy shoot at our neighbors

       at the gas station where N & I buy chips
and loosies after school, we are used to it,

all of us—to crouching low in hopes
       the bullet or the blast will miss us—

       but when the teacher interrupts our quiz
to wheel in a TV cart that groans over the linoleum,

there are few of us who call fear
       a friend within our bodies. The girl

       in front of me is crying because her mother,
who will be safe, who she doesn't know is safe,

works in one of the buildings hit & I am crying
       because my friend is stretching its arms

       around the sky. All throughout the classroom,
children welcome my friend as their own,

make room for it to root. The boy sniper
       will be deemed *irreparable; corrupted* by a judge

       & we will wonder how a boy
could become fear so young, how young

he must have been when fear took root
            for it to grow to overtake him, make

                more of itself. In a few years, children
in this classroom will sit silent in the dark & yet

this might be the last time the room holds grief
            so openly, at once. Our neighbors at the gas station

            will go back to work, will go even while
the snipers are active, since it is on their way

to the work they do because a) they want;
            or because b) they must; or because c) perhaps

            all answers here are true or could
become so. We will get many chances

to tend to the fear that's invasive
            to our bodies now, or not. To root, to uproot,

            to purify, to sow—& the sky
welcomes the embrace & we pull weeds

when they grow & the screen we watch it on
            blinks & the walls come down.

## September Mourning

O limbo of life—
the wings dapple
mourning,
a twitter in the field,
color in the wind,
a spider on feet of purest gossamer.

Trust goes up in flames.

Girders

change

loved ones,

doors strange to touch,

all the lovely times

sinking

in the face of the steely plumes

breaking apart

brilliances
under the jet, so silver and
beautiful—
gone—

the going on
lifting

dreams

competing for truth

for dear life's sake

holding the screams

held together by need.

Give me breath.

Cockleburs on an old man's knees—
roses November leaves—

the memory of this place

catches us
off center

loses hold
and holds to nothing,

the world seeming
seamless
days of glory,

a tapestry
of women and men
dawdling
and scuffling their
shoes, eyeing their toes,

knowing there is nothing to say

that might lighten the load
turning around, coming back, onward,
never to finish telling the story

*numb in the name*
*of the fluttering flag*
*o say can the tattered one*
*defend the fences fenced around*
*and in and through this century of all times*
*the way a baby's wrapped in a shawl or shirt for the*
*tucking into the arms*
*clutching dear life so thin*
*the stubborn holding on*
*a giving in*

# Twine

### After 9/11

I can see the memories twine, strands fray at edges
swing slowly in the wind as tired old hands try to grasp
and hold and tie this twine around any two words
just to keep them together just to hear them make sense
to see children express any kind of understanding
any kind of understanding at all and any kind of hope
that this time the twine is stronger and that this time
it comes from a ball tightly wrapped and waiting, just
waiting for appropriate moments to unwind, just a little bit
just a very little bit at a time—inching out, shyly, slipping
downward in short bursts of length all holding together
all still connected to the ball of twine all the same color
and length of thread all ready to be wrapped and then
tied into a perfect bow, tightly holding the pieces of paper
ashes, and clothing, tightly tying them together in a package
that the children recognize so they can see and say yes!
this holds together, we understand these bundles and
why all this happened and that you can finally share
with twine strong and holding, and understand,
and you can see that too, that the twine is unfurling
in an organized way, not dropping to the floor
like a small worm that will dry out and die upon the
concrete in the sun—no, not heat from the sun, but
spring rain to keep the twine moist and cool
so that it may hold its shape, dry gently, be pulled back
up around the ball, held in place, and then let out again
caught by hands that can help wrap it around these
nests of memory words pulled together, arrayed
on the table for all to see and pray that this time
the twine holds, this time the bundles make sense,
this time the memory twine works and we can all see that
forever tight and strong this memory twine will not break.

# Where We Are

Three a.m., the house a foreign country I wake in,
same language but a different inflection,
a creak on the stair a harbinger,
this jolt into insomnia an alert.

In an etching by Goya, demons perch on a bedpost
and clamor for the sleeper's heart.

Long ago we knelt for prayers
but those children have slept for years,
dreams merging child into beast.
                        Somewhere
a truck explodes and bodies bloom
with the fleshy extravagance of peonies—
                            forgive me,
not petals but a scream settling on entrails,
bone, meat, our betrayals piling in gutters.

It should be obvious where the fault lies,
yet we continue to build there, the structure
collapsing into itself, the century in ruins.
                        Somewhere
a trail remains, linking our inlands,
the path to summers in the mountains
where a halo of hummingbirds
crowns the feeder,
rock hectored by a snow-fed river,
mist from the falls beading our hair.

Moving as we do from the body
and its parochial demands to lessons of love,
you might say we succeed as often as not,
on call even as we sleep.
                        Even as we sleep,
the cry of a puma cracks the night.

# A Carol at Ground Zero

*The people who walked in darkness have seen a great light...*
—Isaiah 9:2

Out of the clear blue of 9-11
from a morning's perfect heaven
on stolen silver wings Satan
fell like lightning rattling
against and shattering
the Windows On The World

And his fire was cast in the sanctuary
of our hearts and in the harbor
Lady Liberty trembled in the dark
surprise of broad daylight
as The Trade Towers crumbled
and their huddled masses were sundered
and scattered in the light of her lamp lifted
beside The Golden Door

And, so, the dead skyscraped mirror
was humbled to the ground
splintered with the cracked reflections
of the thousands of the Just cradled
in the Hand of God testing
them like gold in a crucible

"In the hopes and fears of all the years
met in us tonight. . ." we must stand and be
counted with the dead in the living
flames of the furnace of Faith again
their bodies our minds not lost
but only changed into something wondr'ous
strange their souls shining in a glory

Sweeping through the world in a carol
at Ground Zero its sparks dancing
in a pained radiance skipping

through the rubble choiring
of how the people walking in darkness
must see once more the Great light born

The baby rocked in the ashen creche
and call Him Wonderful Counselor Hero
The Child I Am Who Am The Wounded Healer
burned and ever burning with us
holy embers still smoldering within
the Towers' wreckage pulsing like vigils
of the little fallen fires of the stars

Heaven's very wishes themselves coming
down to Earth seeding with promise
this dark Christmas garden with their
striking beacons wed to deepest Easter Light

# Four Years Later, It's a Deeper Sad

The memorial wall, Virginia Military Institute, our nephew's
plaque flanks the right of the open stairway. On the left
another tablet, his classmate. Two killed in the war in Iraq
honored during their fifteenth college reunion. The chaplain
marches down the flight of steps dressed in formal uniform,
covered in medals and honors. He wears the green beret.

Members of the class gather, some stand in shade,
others in the bright light of this October Sunday.
There are children. But our nephew's are not present
to listen as the chaplain calls their father's name
or hear Taps play by a young cadet behind the wall
overhead. Wind carries the sound.

My brother-in-law's shoulders slump, head hangs,
hands clasp in front of him. His wife's face grimaces,
tears flow, heart pounds visibly in the cavity of her chest.
Red hair rests against the strong arm of their son's roommate.
I cling close to my husband's side. His nephew, the only
living heir, except for those two children none of us see.

Their blonde hair reminds me of baby pictures stored
in my attic of my husband and his brother. Mementos.
Where will they go when we're gone and my in-laws
are dead, too? They've aged these four years, faces drained
as if they've cried the fifty-two months after receiving the news,
their only child bombed in Balad. Where do we go from here?

Up the stairwell, hugging the wall to the road leading out?
Or do we stand and wait for the sun to cast a shadow
in the direction where we must walk?

# September 11

The last time I flew
I stared down at the earth
like a lost traveler
looking for an arrow
marked *This Way*.
I saw nothing but clouds.
Today I was safe in my house
when the stories of all those lives
collapsed
and the film of mine flapped
well past *The End*.
Outside my window
a hummingbird
goes from flower to flower
to flower.

# Time Replaying

### After 9/11

I overslept on a Tuesday in sunny California, arriving at the library late.
I tried to slip through the loading dock, but found my coworkers circling
an old TV just inside the door, the picture rolling up into the fatheaded
box: a plane diving into a skyscraper. Then the news reporter showed us
the second plane disappearing into flames. John, our cataloger, pushed
the antenna arms open while people leaped from windows.

Perched like a toad on a table filled with books, the TV didn't allow
much, so when the towers came down, one then the other rolled
into static—impossible to understand. People running through the
streets covered in heavy dust. A memory of watching footage of
the Beirut bombing on our black and white, tangled with images of
New Yorkers stumbling out of the rubble—differences disguised with
ash—the equalizer of life.

Had I ever thought about the axis of America, the mechanism of
safety cracking? That a plane could disappear completely into a
smoking hole? With the eyeteeth of steel framing visible where the
towers stood, the news reporter started back at the beginning. This
time with circles drawn around planes, around people dropping from
the burning towers, with time to sharpen cellphone footage with
arrows to make hell less obscure.

John slapped the side of the box when the image was gone too long in
static, and this helped us see what happened to America, the old TV
as our center point, our pivot and we oscillated into a national pain. I
closed my eyes for a moment and memory blinked in me:

the rock wall at the swimming hole on Navarro River where I spent
my summers rose into view. In 1984 and I was twelve and impressed
by the high schoolers who cranked AC/DC's "Highway to Hell"
while they flung themselves off a narrow ledge, barely missing the
rocks below. An emerald pool shaded in the afternoon, swallowing
their bright vector into cold, crushing the heat out of them.

I'd never gone to the one hundredth floor in any building, though I climbed a two hundred-foot redwood for a boy in the dark and fog so I could feel his hand guide my hand to the next branch up, dying if I couldn't spend my whole life loving him.

I fought my way back to the surface where John slammed the picture out of static—a skyline of smoke, the towers coming down, one then the other in instant replay.

## Across the Abyss

Join me in imagination
as I become Islamic, the weather-wrinkled
father of my martyred son.

Feel with me
         my fury
as I hold his picture with piercing pride,
belovéd son.
             Feel the screaming
thunder in my skull.
                 Feel
the torment of rage that hollows hours, days,
threatens to be everlasting . . .

till an old friend sees his picture
and drops a tear upon my hand
exploding all—
              into anguish.

Heave with me, grieve with me,
joining our mourning songs

as we breathe the same air
           walk the same land
                   drink the same stream

# In Silence I See

at the 9/11 Memorial

A father's hand brushes his young
daughter's hair into a ponytail.

Through whispers, strangers are asked
to take pictures of friends. Cameras silently

frame where the towers once stood
and it is hard to smile.

Though waterfalls attempt
to replace terror with calmness,

tears flood Ground Zero, still. Between
leaves the sun casts shadows.

　　　On names
a single white rose is laid.

I am here, in silence, trying
to imagine what was then. No longer

removed by miles of television screens
I catch my breath where 2,871 could not

before noticing, just steps away, the dad—
jacket slightly opened—wearing

a red and yellow t-shirt, the "S" stitched
prominently on his chest.

# I Don't Know Her Name

Boss Woman, white apathy breathes dragon fire.
Boss Woman, look into my paleness. See
schoolgirl eyes haunting me since ninth grade.
She never sat on my throne.
I want to amend for predators
devouring diversity and peace.
For those swallowing our planet.
Plagues needing quarantine.
Boss Woman, this faceless machine
force-feeds freedom into graves.
Boss Woman, how can girl, now woman,
still believe in forward together?

Her power takes my breath.

# Bagpipe Parade, NYC, 11 September 2002

We look all day for a parade route,
all night for love. Ours

was immense and then lost
over years and distance, across

our marriages to other people,
so we lie in a hotel bed

in a city where we are unknown;
as my eyelids flutter to a close

as he waits for me to sleep,
a faint wail of pipes stirs us

to part, as we always have,
as we will one day do for good,

and pull our clothes from the pile
where we shed them hours ago,

run outside, ears perked
like hunting dogs in a maze

of buildings like the redwood forest
close to where we met as teenagers,

turn corner after corner until we enter
a sea of people walking—

we tangle through neighborhoods
as the crowd grows, themselves

awoken and lured from living
rooms next to small churches,

streets with balls on stoops,
the tables of any household,

and it goes like this for hours I think, miles I am sure,
but I keep track only of us in this moment

the procession feeding our momentum—
the sky gets lighter yet the sun doesn't shine

until we reach the Hudson, hand in hand,
in view of what will never be again.

## Voice of the Wreckage

      Circle
my smoldering bones,
wrist-hinge and shin. Shine
your false light, searching
for what I am not.
      And when you stagger
upon my lone gold ring, you will
be wedded to absence. I am
a tissue-thin stain
to add to the earth's striata:
bloodfall, breastmilk, body
of little but water, rich vein
of memory you are measuring.

      So I will tell you:
one sharp breath was all we took away.

Now my sigh, gauze lung in the leaves,
feeds your zeal for flame. And when
the last smoke lifts, filled
with flesh, I leave you
      hungered.

# Erasures for 9/11

An eastern screech owl in the crevice of a tree
A walking stick insect on a leaf.

Deer gliding through the edge of the woods
A cria dropped in the tall grass.

Birth and rebirth wear many disguises
And outlive death.

Take a deep breath:
Sunrise will come, and deeper love.
See Icarus rising from the green water.

## The Boy of Steel

Once upon a time, as the news began
the count, while New York City sifted the rubble,

two days after the towers showered down,
I bowed over the galleys of a children's book,
and I got back to my work. My son,

then two years and four months old,
and all of three feet tall, entered the kitchen
where I'd spread out my craft on the table,
like debris across an empty field. No.

He did not simply enter, per se;
he flourished into the room, red cape first,
dressed, as he was, in his Superman costume,
the kind with the built-in muscles and six-pack abs.
His outfit, a hand-me-down, two sizes too big,

his face deathly serious, his legs locked and strong.
Hands on hips. Lips pursed. Eyes on alert,
and scanning the kitchen for danger
as if to say, I've got you, Daddy. Gut-struck.
His innocence crashed into me. I swayed,
and the force was transferred to the structure,

absorbed and dissipated in such a way
that eventually the skyscraper righted itself.
Like a spindly willow or an awkward youth,
the building receives the wind's abuse and bends,
because wind is only bluster, and life goes on
between the gusts. The willow whips upright,
its dignity intact, and nothing to prove. Ta-da!

Over the years, I've watched my boy-of-steel suffer
surprise attacks, dumbly sway and right himself,
and never see them coming. Whatever now pierces
his armor of adulthood is left as a memorial inside.
My son, grown twenty-two years old and all of six feet tall
has now left home to stand on his own in the world,
conspicuously open for business, as always,
rising up through the scar tissue, an easy target;

in a world whose capability to destroy has far outpaced
its capacity to comprehend how all destruction
is self-destruction; a world whose right hand holds the gun
and will shoot the left hand, even when it is unarmed.
My son could not keep his head down if he tried.
The charred and mangled planes remain.
The broken bits of them are left inside
to set off future suspicions and metal detectors.
And me? I'm still just Clark, the man of flesh.

That's why I'll start another children's book today,
while near three thousand mortals molder in their tombs.
The planet has efficient ancient ways
to cover over self-inflicted wounds.

# 1.5°C

(the global-temperature-rise limit required to prevent large-scale
suffering, according to the Intergovernmental Panel on Climate Change)

Where does that shake
in Mama's voice
come from?

What will our daughters do
with all this rain,

all that fracked
water flooding the Gulf?

How long before
the tipping point?

Is the future
a burning throat?

A boat with no home?

A hemlock dead

to the crown?

To be
hungry,

to live

underground—

bombs
falling on bombed-out
houses—

has always
been present tense

but in America we are
still brutally innocent.

The power flickers
on & off.
                    The lights

flicker & then stay
off.

    We've been dreaming

our own demise
for too long now,

but my girl?

            She searches
the internet
for inspirational sayings.

            She asks
how much
college costs.

            She stands on her toes,
to see how close
we are in height

& imagines the forest

            before the hemlocks died,

            before the chainsaw

found it, before

temperature shifts
& weed killers

silenced the insects

silenced the birds.

## Tuesday Morning, English 11

Chatter and lockers slamming,
taking the roll, announcements,

and, finally, we read from "Song of Myself":
"Agonies are one of my change of garments."

The intercom: "Teachers, turn on your TVs."

The first tower collapses,
and I remember the observation deck, I feel
as if I am balancing on a wing
over Manhattan, the sunlit river, the ocean,

I think of the crowded stairs, the firemen climbing,
I sit down, my knees, the girders giving way.
Then the second—

Then the mantra is born, a reporter
pronouncing, his colleagues repeating:
"a day when everything changed!"

As if the universe were transformed
from the subatomic to the galactic, everything
rippling with strangeness and dread.

But it's not true, it misses the mark,
one story erasing another.
I turn it off, I speak of what lives on—

They want to continue, and I try to read,
"I am the mash'd fireman with breast bone broken."

A volunteer picks it up, she concludes,
"The kneeling crowd fades with the light of the torches."

# For Bobi Wine

Robert Kyagulanyi Ssentamu, known by his stage name, Bobi Wine, is a Ugandan politician, singer, actor and businessman. He participated in the 2021 Ugandan presidential election. where he lost to incumbent Yoweri Museveni, a result which Kyagulanyi and a large section of the public strongly refuted.

Bobi Wine
Bobi Wine
I have closed my eyes
& dreamt of leaving America

Bobi Wine
I am writing to tell you this

that
I woke up this morning and I was
still
in America

over there
they have turned out the lights
but over here
I can still see Kampala
all of Uganda
what Museveni has done
they have turned off the radio in Uganda

but I have only just begun singing
*Bobi Wine from*
*Uganda*
*Kampala*
*Uganda*

You crown your own head with love
sending power over to the people
you know the people are the power

every night before I pray
I wrap you in between my palms
so
why don't you
lift your head Bobi
over Museveni
over all of them
until all of parliament is singing
of Bobi Wine
the Ghetto King
the Pearl of Parliament
the Freedom Drum from Kampala Slum

Why should we say free Bobi Wine?
When Bobi Wine has showed us
what it means to be free

In Kampala I hear bells ringing
and even they are saying
*Bo-bi*
*Bo-bi*
*Bo-biiiiiii*

## Trope

a vote for   bush
a vote for   genocide
all those culpable in the late war
left bodies bloated in streets
paved fresh   your new boots
that lanvin ad lying all sleek and
sooty and gloss along fifth avenue
pretty morning after the smoke
jets dropping same on soccer kids
weaving through your phobias seen
that man took the late shift
found around fifty-two cents
underfunding himself for your heels
still clicking and clicking
now see you scrolling enacting
quiz for this that new genocide
which is what is barriers
gliding by mass revolutions
relaxed into colonization borders
at night slide in using the sacred heart
in defense in lieu of you asking
refuse or redo or renew?
believing that this is reformation
or else perpetually revalue
as W keeps coming for me
keeps dropping down on me
some sort of strange sandstorm
tricking you raising me
as I ask you to explore me
but you exploit and lay down
another tread and get in your car
and do the same thing

# In Flight

We board fast in order to miss the storm. Back near the gate, a man had thrashed and flailed on the carpet, foaming from the mouth, circled by EMTs who spoke slowly and too loud. Fast food workers peered over their counters. The men at the bar chuckled uneasily. *You have to be careful,* said the lady who sold me an apple, *They can swallow their tongues.* The man shrieked and the hair on the back of my neck stood up. In ancient days, demons would have been blamed, these convulsions proof of the dark struggle for our souls. Our plane shudders through thunderheads, airborne by sorcery I don't understand. We've beaten the front. Across the aisle, a woman underlines her book in pencil adding emphasis to words she's already highlighted in acid yellow. One row ahead another woman sleeps, slumped over the pillow of her coat bunched on her tray table, her mouth soft and open. Between the crack in the seats in front of me, football players scramble across the screen of an iPad held by a man's hairy hand. The woman with the book has perfect, squared nails painted glossy red. I try to see what she's so carefully studying. A figure crouches on her book cover, inside a circle with a slash. *How to S_____Proof Your Home,* I make out. *Squirrel?* Once I had the same trouble when a nesting mother intent on shelter gnawed her way into the attic and I could hear her scratch in the walls. Now, the attendant delivers drinks to those still awake. The smell of scotch. The figure on the book is holding a spear, no, a pitchfork, like the Hormel devil. Satan! Vanna, I'd like to solve the puzzle, she's trying to *Satan-Proof* her house. What steps would you take, I wonder, and think of ropes of garlic. No, that's vampires. She doesn't look crazy, quietly marking another passage of note. The fragile magic of a list to tick, a murmur of words. Later, after we're safely home, I'll learn the storm we skirted flung tornadoes here and there. Black thumbs rubbing out houses.

# Contributor Biographies

**Robert Abbate** teaches English and ethics at Rowan-Cabarrus Community College in Concord, North Carolina. His first full-length poetry manuscript, *Courage of Straw*, was a finalist for the Bright Hill Press Poetry Book Contest in 2005, and a finalist for the John Ciardi Poetry Prize from BkMk Press in 2006. Robert's poem "Tishbite Pottery Fragments" was a finalist for the 2007 James Hearst Poetry Award from *North American Review*. Main Street Rag published *Courage of Straw* in March of 2010. "*Ars Memorativa*" is from *Courage of Straw*, Main Street Rag Publishing Company, Charlotte, North Carolina, 2010.

**Anthony S. Abbott** is the author of eight prize-winning books of poetry, two novels, and four books of literary criticism. He is the recipient of the North Carolina Award in Literature and a member of the North Carolina Literary Hall of Fame. He served as the Charles A. Dana Professor of English Emeritus at Davidson College. "This Innocent Sky" is from *If Words Could Save Us*, Lorimer Press, Davidson, North Carolina, 2011.

**Dr. Diya Abdo** is a Palestinian professor of English and Women's/Gender Studies, writer, and activist. She is the founder and director of the national campus-based refugee resettlement program Every Campus A Refuge. She is also the Director of UNC-Greensboro's Center for New North Carolinians. She lives with her family in Greensboro, North Carolina.

**Kathy Ackerman** has never served in the military or on the front lines of anything but education, but she is profoundly grateful to all who sacrifice(d). Her books include *A Quarrel of Atoms* (Lena Shull Poetry Book Award); *Coal River Road; The Heart of Revolution;* and three chapbooks.

Among **Betty Adcock**'s volumes of poetry are *The Difficult Wheel, Intervale: New and Selected Poems*, and *Slantwise*. She is the recipient of the North Carolina Award in Literature, two Pushcart Prizes, a Guggenheim Fellowship, and a number of other prizes. She was Writer-in-Residence and taught for many years at Meredith College.

**Anjail Rashida Ahmad's** poems have appeared in *Midlands, African American Review, Black Scholar,* and *Ark/Angel Review.* She is the author of the volumes *Necessary Kindling* and *Reunion: Poems.* For years, she directed the Creative Writing Program at North Carolina A&T State University.

**Malaika King Albrecht** is serving as the inaugural Heart of Pamlico Poet Laureate. She's the author of four poetry books. Her most recent is *The Stumble Fields* (Main Street Rag, 2020). She's the founding editor of *Redheaded Stepchild,* an online magazine that only accepts poems that have been rejected elsewhere.

**Debra Allbery's** most recent collection is *Fimbul-Winter* (Four Way Books, 2010) which won the Grub Street National Book Prize in Poetry. She has received two fellowships from the National Endowment for the Arts, the Starrett Prize, and a Discovery/*The Nation* prize, among other awards. She directs the MFA Program for Writers at Warren Wilson College. "The Wakeful Bird Sings Darkling" is from *Fimbul-Winter,* Four Way Books, 2010.

**Threa Almontaser** is the author of the poetry collection, *The Wild Fox of Yemen* (Graywolf Press), selected by Harryette Mullen for the 2020 Walt Whitman Award from The Academy of American Poets. She is the recipient of awards from the Civitella Ranieri Foundation in Italy, the National Endowment for the Arts, the Fulbright Program, and elsewhere. She earned her MFA and TESOL certification from North Carolina State University. "Home Security after 9/11" is from *The Wild Fox of Yemen,* Graywolf Press.

**Darnell Arnoult's** works include the novel, *Sufficient Grace,* and poetry collections, *What Travels with Us* and *Galaxie Wagon.* She's received the SIBA Poetry Book of the Year Prize, the Weatherford Award, the Thomas and Lillie D. Chaffin Award, and the Mary Frances Hobson Award in Arts and Letters. Arnoult lives in Mebane, North Carolina.

**Sally Atkins,** professor emerita and founding coordinator of the Expressive Arts Program at Appalachian State University, and professor of expressive arts at the European Graduate School, has been honored both for her teaching and her research, including most recently, *Poetry in Expressive Arts Therapy* (2020), co-authored with Margo Fuchs Knill. "This Thing Rising between Us" is from *Picking Clean the Bones*, Parkway Publishers, Blowing Rock, North Carolina, 2005.

**Margaret Boothe Baddour** is the author of *A Murmuration of Purrs, Easy Magic*, and *Scheherazade*. Among her awards are the North Carolina Poet Laureate Award and the Charlotte Writers Award. Her poems have been published in numerous literary magazines, and she has taught Creative Writing and directed Readers Theater for all ages. "No Bloodshed during Snowfall" is from *Scheherazade*, St. Andrews University Press, 2009.

**John Balaban** is the author of thirteen books of poetry and prose. His most recent book of poetry is *Empires* (Copper Canyon Press, 2019), which begins with "A Finger." He lives in Cary, North Carolina. "A Finger" is from *Empires*, Copper Canyon Press, 2019.

**Joan Barasovska** lives in Chapel Hill, North Carolina. She cohosts a poetry series at Flyleaf Books and serves on the Board of the North Carolina Poetry Society. *Birthing Age* (Finishing Line Press) is her first book. Joan was nominated for Best of the Net and a Pushcart Prize in 2020.

**Sam Barbee** has a new book, *Uncommon Book of Prayer* (2021, Main Street Rag). His poems recently appeared in *Poetry South*, and *Asheville Poetry Review*. His collection, *That Rain We Needed* (Press 53, 2016 ), was nominated for the Roanoke-Chowan Award as one of North Carolina's best poetry collections of 2016. He is a Pushcart Prize nominee.

**Tina Barr**'s most recent book, *Green Target*, won the Barrow Street Press Poetry Prize and the Brockman-Campbell Award. Previous books include *The Gathering Eye*, winner of the Tupelo Press Editor's Award, and *Kaleidoscope*. She's received fellowships from the NEA, The Tennessee Arts Commission, & the Pennsylvania Council on the Arts. "Threat" is from *Green Target*, Barrow Street Press.

**Gerald Barrax** is the author of a number of poetry volumes, including *Leaning Against the Sun*, nominated for the Pulitzer Prize and the National Book Award. He is the recipient of the 2009

North Carolina Award in Literature, and is a member of the North Carolina Literary Hall of Fame. In 1997, he retired after a long, distinguished teaching career in North Carolina State University's MFA Program in Creative Writing.

**Joseph Bathanti**, former Poet Laureate of North Carolina (2012-14) and recipient of the North Carolina Award in Literature, is author of seventeen books. Bathanti is McFarlane Family Distinguished Professor of Interdisciplinary Education at Appalachian State University. He served as the 2016 Charles George VA Medical Center Writer-in-Residence in Asheville, North Carolina, and is the co-founder of the Medical Center's Creative Writing Program.

**Ronald H. Bayes** is the Emeritus Distinguished Professor of Literature and Creative Writing and Writer-in-Residence at St. Andrews University in Laurinburg, North Carolina, where he had a long and legendary career. He is a member of the North Carolina Literary Hall of Fame and recipient of the North Carolina Award in Literature. He is the author of numerous books. "Going South" is from *The Collected Poems of Ronald H. Bayes*, St. Andrews University Press, 2015.

**Michael Beadle** is a poet, author, writer-in-residence, and avid naturalist living in Raleigh, North Carolina. His latest poetry collection is *Beasts of Eden* (Press 53). His poems have been featured in anthologies, festivals, schools, churches, restaurants, a cookbook, a city trolley, and the North Carolina Zoo.

**Jeffery Beam**'s latest works are *Spectral Pegasus/Dark Movements*, the virtual *Don't Forget Love*, and J*onathan Williams: Lord of Orchards*. He has collaborated with numerous composers including Daniel Thomas Davis, Lee Hoiby, Steven Serpa, and Tony Solitro. He and his husband of forty-one years live at Golgonooza at Frog Level, Hillsborough, NC. "A Stone Falling, a Falling Stone" is from A *Time of Trial: Beyond the Terror of 9/11* anthology, Toronto, Canada: Hidden Brook Press, 2001.

**Peter Blair** has written three full-length books of poems, most recently, *Farang*, published by Autumn House Press. He lives in Charlotte, North Carolina, and teaches at the University of North Carolina at Charlotte. "The Day after the Coup" is from *Farang*, from Autumn House Press, 2010.

**Kim Blum-Hyclak**'s poems and essays have appeared in *The Petigru Review*, her poetry has been published in *Iodine* and *Kakalak*, and her short stories have appeared in *moonShine review*. Kim's first poetry collection, *In the Garden of Life and Death: A Mother and Daughter Walk*, was published by Main Street Rag Publishing Company. Her first novel is looking for a home and her second is still under construction. Kim is a co-editor for *Kakalak*.

North Carolina Poet Laureate, 2010—2012, **Cathy Smith Bowers'** poems have appeared widely in publications such as *The Atlantic Monthly*, *The Georgia Review*, *Poetry*, *The Southern Review*, *The Kenyon Review*, and *Ploughshares*. Her first book, *The Love That Ended Yesterday in Texas*, was the inaugural winner of The Texas Tech University Press First Book Competition. Her fifth book, *The Collected Poems of Cathy Smith Bowers* (Press 53) won the 2014 SIBA Award for Poetry. In March 2017, she was inducted into the South Carolina Author's Hall of Fame. She teaches in Queens University of Charlotte low-residency MFA program.

**Kevin Boyle** is the author of two books: *A Home for Wayward Girls* (New Issues Poetry Prize) and *Astir* (Jacar Press). His poems have appeared in journals, including *Hollins Critic*, *North American Review*, *Pleiades*, *Prairie Schooner* and *Virginia Quarterly Review*. He grew up in Philadelphia and now teaches at Elon University. "Western Chant" was first published in *Natural Bridge*.

**Norma Bradley**, poet/multi-media artist, has shared her love of poetry & visual art in schools and rehabilitation centers for thirty years, and as a participant in the North Carolina Visiting Artists Program. She's been published in *Avocet, Great Smokies Review, Jewish Literary Journal, Snapdragon: A Journal of Art & Healing, Speckled Trout Review, Kakalak,* and *Train River*. Her chapbook, *Ghosts Rip Free*, was recently published.

A North Carolina native from the rural-back-woods-fishing community of Hampstead, **Earl Sherman Braggs** is a UC Foundation and Battle Professor of English at the University of Tennessee at Chattanooga. Braggs is the author of fourteen collections of poetry. Among his many awards are the Anhinga Poetry Prize, and the Jack Kerouac International Literary Prize.

**Jeannette Cabanis-Brewin**'s poetry has appeared in *The Nomad, Atlanta Review, Appalachian Heritage, Great Smokies Review, Notes from the Gean,* and several anthologies, including *The Gift of Experience* (*Atlanta Review*, 2005), *Immigration, Emigration, Diversity* (Chapel Hill Press, 2005), and *The Moveable Nest* (Helicon Press, 2007). Her chapbook, *Patriate,* won the 2007 Longleaf Press Open Chapbook Competition.

**Sally Bucker** taught at Peace College and edited *Our Words, Our Ways: Reading and Writing in North Carolina* (1991), and *Word and Witness: 100 Years of North Carolina Poetry* (1999). She also authored the collections: *Strawberry Harvest* (1986), *Collateral Damage* (2008), and *Nineteen Visions of Christmas* (2011). She was the recipient of the Ragan-Rubin Award, the R. Hunt Parker Award, the Sam Ragan Award, and the City of Raleigh Arts Commission Medal of Arts and others.

**Kathryn Stripling Byer**, recipient of the North Carolina Award in Literature, and member of the North Carolina Literary Hall of Fame, served as North Carolina's first woman Poet Laureate, from 2005 until 2010. Among her award-winning books are *The Girl in the Midst of the Harvest, Wildwood Flower, Black Shawl, Catching Light, Coming to Rest,* and *Descent.* "Safe" is from the chapbook *Wake,* Spring Street Editions, 2003.

Formerly a magazine and newspaper journalist, **Ann Campanella** is the author of two memoirs, *Motherhood: Lost and Found* and *Celiac Mom,* and four collections of poetry. Her writing has appeared in literary journals, newspapers and magazines around the world. A graduate of Davidson College, she calls North Carolina home. "Contractions: September 11, 2001" is from *What Flies Away,* Main Street Rag Publishing Co., 2006

After four decades of creating large public sculpture, **Maryrose Carroll** had to quit. Her books are *Beats Me: Love, Poetry, Censorship from Chicago to Appalachia* (2015), *Conversations with a Dead Lover* (2017), *Tales from Beaver Dams* (2018), *Love Poems~Poemas de Amor* (2020), and *The Secret of Contentment* (2021).

In 2004, **Fred Chappell** retired after teaching forty years in the English Department of UNC-Greensboro. He is guilty of thirty-odd books of poetry, fiction, and literary commentary. Various awards have fallen on him. His wife Susan has made gratitude one of the major parts of his life, as have his son, daughter-in-law, friends, animals, neighbors and colleagues. His latest book of verse is *As If It Were* from Louisiana State University Press (2019); his novel, *A Shadow of All Light*, was published by Tor Books in 2016.

**Richard Chess** is the author of four books of poetry, the most recent of which is *Love Nailed to the Doorpost*. He is the former director of the Center for Jewish Studies at UNC Asheville and Emeritus Professor.

**Elisabeth Lewis Corley**'s poems have appeared in *Michigan Quarterly Review, Southern Poetry Review, Hyperion, Carolina Quarterly, Feminist Studies, BigCityLit, New Haven Review, Cold Mountain Review, Consequence*, and others. She holds an MFA in poetry from the Warren Wilson Program for Writers and a BA with Highest Honors in Poetry from the University of North Carolina at Chapel Hill.

**Thomas Rain Crowe** is an internationally-published and recognized author of more than thirty books, including the multi-award-winning nonfiction nature memoir *Zoro's Field: My Life in the Appalachian Woods*; a book of essays and articles titled *The End of Eden (Writings of an Environmental Activist)*; and a collection of place-based poems titled *Crack Light*. He is founder and publisher of New Native Press. He is and has been on the boards of several environmental conservation organizations in Western North Carolina over the last forty years.

**Christopher Davis** is the author of four collections of poetry: *The Tyrant of the Past and the Slave of the Future*; *The Patriot*; *A History of the Only War*; and, most recently, *Oath*. A graduate of the Iowa Writer's Workshop, he is a professor of creative writing at UNC Charlotte. "Idol" first appeared in *Hawaii Review*, Issue 83, Spring 2016.

**Benito del Pliego** is a Spanish-born North Carolinian poet, translator, and researcher with a long record of publications, among them ten original books of poetry. He was included in Forrest Gander's anthology *Panic Cure* (2013). *Fábula/Fable* was published in a bilingual edition in 2016. He teaches at Appalachian State University.

**M. Scott Douglass** lives outside Charlotte, North Carolina. He is Publisher and Managing Editor at Main Street Rag Publishing Company, an award-winning graphic artist and poet, a Pushcart Prize nominee, and a grant recipient from the North Carolina Arts & Science Council. His most recent book: *Just Passing Through* (Paycock Press, 2017).

**Hilda Downer** grew up in Bandana in Western North Carolina. A long-term member of the Southern Appalachian Writers Cooperative and the North Carolina Writers Conference, she has an MFA from Vermont College. She has two books of poetry: *Bandana Creek* and *Sky Under the Roof* from Bottom Dog Press. "Message to the Unborn" was first published in *Pine Mountain Sand & Gravel*.

**Julia Nunnally Duncan** is a native of Western North Carolina and author of ten books of poetry and prose. She spent over thirty years teaching English at her local community college. Retired now, she concentrates on her writing and enjoys spending time with her husband Steve and their daughter Annie.

**Brenda Flanagan** is the Edward Armfield Professor of English at Davidson College and the recipient of the Hunter Hamilton Love of Teaching Award. Her books of fiction are: *You Alone Are Dancing*; *Allah in The Islands*; and *In Praise of Island Women & Other Crimes*. She is the author of the play, *When the Jumbiebird Calls*.

**Charles Fort** is the author of six books of poetry and ten chapbooks, including *The Town Clock Burning*, and *We Did Not Fear the Father*. His work has been featured in forty-five anthologies and appeared in *The Best American Poetry* in 2001, 2003 and 2016. Fort is Distinguished Emeritus Endowed Professor at the University of Nebraska at Kearney and Founder of the Wendy Fort Foundation Theater of Fine Arts. "In a Just and Miniature World" is from *We Did Not Fear the Father: New and Selected Poems*, Red Hen Press, 2012.

**Janice Moore Fuller** has published four poetry collections, including *Séance*, winner of the Oscar Arnold Young Award for the outstanding North Carolina poetry book. Her plays and libretti, including a stage adaptation of Faulkner's novel, *As I Lay Dying,* have been produced in North Carolina, Minneapolis, Estonia, and France. "This Whistling Is for You There in the Dark" is from *Sex Education,* Iris Press, Knoxville, TN, 2004.

**Jaki Shelton Green**, ninth Poet Laureate of North Carolina, is the first African American and third woman to be appointed as the North Carolina Poet Laureate. She is a 2019 Academy of American Poet Laureate Fellow, 2014 North Carolina Literary Hall of Fame Inductee, 2009 North Carolina Piedmont Laureate appointee, and 2003 recipient of the North Carolina Award for Literature.

**Bill Griffin** is a family physician (retired) in rural North Carolina. Poetry may not have saved his patients, but poetry has certainly saved him. Bill's poems have appeared widely, including *Tar River Poetry, Southern Poetry Review, and North Carolina Literary Review*. His most recent collection is *Riverstory : Treestory* (The Orchard Street Press 2018). "Every Child" is from *Crossing the River*, Main Street Rag Publishing Company, 2017.

**Allison Adelle Hedge Coke** came of age in North Carolina working fields, factories, waters. A sharecropper by her mid-teens, she worked manual labor, until nearly thirty years of age, when disabilities precluded continuation. For the past thirty years, she's worked in literary activism, intervention, and bibliotherapy/narrative medicine.

**Thomas Heffernan**, born on Cape Cod, grew up there and in Boston. Awards include The Sam Ragan Fine Arts Award, Roanoke-Chowan Award for Poetry (for *The Liam Poems)*, and the Kusamakura Grand Prize for Haiku. He has taught at North Carolina State University, St. Andrews University, UNC-Pembroke, and universities in England and Japan. His latest book is *Working Voices*. After first appearing on the NC Arts Council website, "Remembering 9/11: Soon It Will Be Ten Years, Lines Written on Sept. 4, 2011" was republished in *St. Andrews Review* and in the anthology *Ezra's Book*, Clemson University Press, 2019.

**Marylin Hervieux** has numerous publications including in *Tar River Poetry* and *The North Carolina Literary Review*, where she was nominated for a Pushcart Prize. She's been a Finalist and Honorable Mention in the James Applewhite Poetry Prize Competition. She's taught poetry workshops to special needs groups as the recipient of an Orange County Arts Commission Artist Project Grant.

**Irene Blair Honeycutt** has published four poetry books, the most recent: *Beneath the Bamboo Sky* (Main Street Rag, 2017). She founded Central Piedmont Community College's Spring Literary Festival (Sensoria). She lives in Indian Trail, North Carolina, remains active in the writing community, and is working on her fifth poetry manuscript.

**John Hoppenthaler**'s books of poetry are *Domestic Garden*; *Anticipate the Coming Reservoir*; and *Lives of Water*, all with Carnegie Mellon UP. He has co-edited a volume of essays on the poetry of Jean Valentine, *This-World Company*. He is a Professor of Creative Writing and Literature at East Carolina University. "A Jar of Rain" is from *Anticipate the Coming Reservoir*, Carnegie Mellon UP, 2008.

**Holly Iglesias** has written three poetry collections, *Sleeping Things*; *Angles of Approach*; and *Souvenirs of a Shrunken World*; and a critical work, *Boxing Inside the Box: Women's Prose Poetry*. Her awards include fellowships from the National Endowment for the Arts, the North Carolina Arts Council, and the Massachusetts Cultural Council.

**Fred Joiner** is a poet based in Chapel Hill, North Carolina. He is the poet Laureate of Carrboro, North Carolina, and an Academy of American Poets Laureate Fellow. His work has appeared or is forthcoming in *Obsidian*; *All the Songs We Sing* (Blair); *FURIOUS FLOWER: Seeding the Future of African American Poetry* (Northwestern University Press); and other publications. Most recently, Joiner guest-curated an exhibition (Micro/Macro) of the 2021 Master of Fine Arts in Studio Art graduates at UNC-Chapel Hill for The Ackland Art Museum. A version of "Sovereignty" appeared in *The Next Verse Poets Mixtape Volume One: the 4x4*, Central Square Press, 2016

**Paul Jones**'s work has appeared in *Poetry, Triggerfish Critical Review, Broadkill Review, 2River View*, and anthologies, including *Best American Erotic Poems (1800–Present)*. He was recently nominated for two Pushcart Prizes and two Best of the Web Awards. His chapbook is *What the Welsh and Chinese Have in Common.*

**Debra Kaufman** is the author of the poetry collections, *God Shattered*; *Delicate Thefts*; *The Next Moment*; and *A Certain Light*; as well as three chapbooks and many monologues and short plays. She is working on her fifth full-length play. Her most recent poems appeared in *Poetry East, North Carolina Literary Review*, and *Triggerfish*. She produced *Illuminated Dresses*, a series of monologues by women, in 2019.

**Katie Kehoe** is a poet-librarian who has published with *Salt Hill, Boudin, The Indianapolis Review, Bayou Magazine, Appalachian Journal*, and elsewhere. She was a finalist for the North Carolina State poetry contest (2019) and nominated for a Pushcart Prize (2020). She holds an MFA from the University of North Carolina at Greensboro.

**Kathryn Kirkpatrick** is Professor of English at Appalachian State University where she teaches environmental literature, animal studies, and Irish studies from an ecofeminist perspective. She is the author of seven books of poetry, including collections addressing female embodiment, climate change, human illness, and non-human animals (*Unaccountable Weather*, 2011; and *Our Held Animal Breath*, 2012). *The Fisher Queen: New & Selected Poems* (Salmon Press, 2019) was awarded the North Carolina Literary & Historical Association's Roanoke-Chowan Award for Poetry.

**Stephen Knauth**'s poetry collections include *The River I Know You By* and *Twenty Shadows*, both from Four Way Books. His work has appeared in *Ploughshares, FIELD, North American Review, Virginia Quarterly Review*, and *Poetry Daily*, among others. He has held fellowships from the NEA and the North Carolina Arts Council. "Lament" was first published in *Water~Stone Review*.

**Carrie Knowles** has published five novels: *Lillian's Garden*; *Ashoan's Rug*; *A Garden Wall in Provence*; *The Inevitable Past*; *A Musical Affair*; and a collection of short stories, *Black Tie Optional*. She also writes a personal perspective column for *Psychology Today*: "Shifting Forward." Carrie was the 2014 North Carolina Piedmont Laureate.

Pulitzer Prize finalist **Dorianne Laux**'s most recent collection is *Only As the Day Is Long: New and Selected Poems*, W.W. Norton. She is also author of *The Book of Men*, winner of the Paterson Poetry Prize; and *Facts about the Moon*, winner of the Oregon Book Award. She teaches poetry at North Carolina State University and Pacific University. In 2020, Laux was elected a Chancellor of the Academy of American Poets. "Blossom" is from the chapbook, *Salt*, from The Field Office, 2020.

**Sarah Lindsay**, a Lannan Foundation fellowship recipient, is the author most recently of *Debt to the Bone-Eating Snotflower*. She is also the author of *Primate Behavior*, Grove Atlantic, 1997. She works as a copy editor in Greensboro, North Carolina. "Nachtmusik" is from *Primate Behavior*, Grove Atlantic, New York City, New York, 1997.

**Tonya Holy Elk Locklear**, an enrolled member of the Oglala Sioux Tribe of Pine Ridge, South Dakota, with kinship ties to the Lumbee Tribe of North Carolina, grew up in Southeastern North Carolina. Her poetry is themed around land, kinship, and food while reminding readers of the importance of preserving Native American culture and identity through oral history traditions.

**Zachary Lunn** served two tours in Iraq as a medic with the 505th Parachute Infantry Regiment. His writing appears in *Slate*, *Oxford American*, *The Missouri Review*, and elsewhere. He works as a park ranger in North Carolina. "Fort Bragg" previously appeared in *Oxford American* as "Fort Bragg Winter" in a slightly different version.

**Peter Makuck**'s poems have appeared in *The Hudson Review*, *Poetry* and *The Sewanee Review*. In 1988 he received the Brockman Award, given annually for the best collection of poetry by a North Carolinian, and the Charity Randall Citation from the International Poetry Forum. *Mandatory Evacuation* (BOA Editions, 2017) is his seventh volume of poetry. "Letter to Bill Heyen" is from *Mandatory Evacuation*.

**Sebastian Matthews** is the author of *Beyond Repair: Living in a Fractured State*, out from Red Hen Press in 2020. His collage novel, *The Life & Times of American Crow*, is due out from Red Hen Press in the spring of 2022.

**Rebecca McClanahan**'s eleventh book is *In the Key of New York City: A Memoir in Essays*. Her work has appeared in *Best American Essays, Best American Poetry, Georgia Review, Gettysburg Review, Kenyon Review*, and numerous anthologies. She has received two Pushcart prizes, the Wood Prize from *Poetry*, and the Glasgow Award in Nonfiction. "Early Morning, Downtown 1 Train" was first published in *The Georgia Review*.

**Michael McFee** is the author or editor of sixteen books, most recently *We Were Once Here: Poems* (Carnegie Mellon University Press, 2017) and *Appointed Rounds: Essays* (Mercer University Press, 2018). He teaches poetry writing at UNC-Chapel Hill. In November 2018, he received the North Carolina Award for Literature. An earlier version of "STOP" (as "March 21, 2003") was published in *Hudson Review*.

Author of *The Woman in Happy Dollar* (Finishing Line Press), **Doug McHargue** has been a finalist for the North Carolina Poetry Society's Poet Laureate Award. Her poems were a part of the Hickory Museum of Art's Ekphrastic Poetry Series, and (pre-Pandemic) she was a regular reader at Poetry Hickory.

**Kevin McIlvoy**'s poems appear in *Consequence, Willow Springs, Olney, Barzakh, River Heron Review, LEON, The Georgia Review*, and other magazines. For twenty-seven years he was editor in chief of the literary magazine *Puerto del Sol*. He taught in the Warren Wilson College MFA Program in Creative Writing from 1987 to 2019, and as a Regents Professor of Creative Writing in the New Mexico State University MFA Program from 1981 to 2008. "Let Us Draw Near" was first published in *Scoundrel Time* journal, September 2020.

**Rose McLarney**'s collections of poetry are *Forage* and *Its Day Being Gone* (Penguin) and *The Always Broken Plates of Mountains* (Four Way Books). She is co-editor of *Southern Humanities Review* and *A Literary Field Guide to Southern Appalachia* (University of Georgia Press) and an Associate Professor at Auburn University. "Winter Hard" is from *Forage*, Penguin, 2019.

Part of a Southern literary family known as the "writing Rosses," **Heather Ross Miller** is the author of many books, including a collection of linked narrative poems titled *Lumina: A Town of Voices* that features the old aluminum-smelting town of Badin, North Carolina, where she grew up; and *Women Disturbing the Peace*, winner of the 2018 Roanoke Chowan Award in Poetry. She is retired from Washington & Lee University, after a long and distinguished teaching career.

**Lenard D. Moore** is an internationally acclaimed poet and anthologist, whose literary works have appeared in more than fifteen countries and have been translated into more than twelve languages. Moore is a U.S. Army Veteran. He is author of *The Geography of Jazz* (Blair, 2020), and editor of *All the Songs We Sing* (Blair, 2020).

**Janice Townley Moore** won first prize in the 2009 Press 53 Open Awards for Poetry, judged by Kathryn Stripling Byer. Her poems have appeared in *Georgia Review, Southern Poetry Review, Poetry East, Shenandoah,* and *Teaching the Robins,* her chapbook. Retired from Young Harris College, she lives in Hayesville, North Carolina.

**Robert Morgan** has published several volumes of poetry, most recently *Dark Energy* (2015) and nine works of fiction, including *Gap Creek* (1999) and *Chasing the North Star* (2016). His nonfiction work includes *Lions of the West* (2011). A native of Western North Carolina, he has taught at Cornell since 1971.

**Ricardo Nazario-Colón** is a cofounder of the Affrilachian Poets and former mentor in the Gilbert-Chappell Distinguished Poet Series of North Carolina Western Region. He is the author of *The Recital,* Winged City Press, 2011; and *Of Jíbaros and Hillbillies,* Plain View Press, 2011. He currently serves as the Chief Diversity Officer at Western Carolina University. "Up North" is from *Of Jíbaros and Hillbillies.*

**Valerie Nieman**'s recent collection, *Leopard Lady: A Life in Verse,* debuted at the Coney Island Museum. Her poetry has appeared widely, including the anthologies *Eyes Glowing at the Edge of the Woods* and *Ghost Fishing: An Eco-Justice Poetry Anthology.* Also a novelist, she has held NEA and state fellowships. "The Knife, Now" was first published in *Change 7,* Winter 2021.

**Ione (Tootsie) O'Hara** taught English as a Second Language at Central Piedmont Community College and UNC-Charlotte. She has facilitated poetry workshops, volunteered as a writing teacher in elementary schools, and has been awarded an Arts & Science Regional Artist Grant. Her work has been nominated for a Pushcart Prize, and her chapbook is *A Passing Certainty.*

**Alan Michael Parker** has written nine collections of poems and four novels. Houchens Professor of English at Davidson College, his writing has appeared in *The New Republic, The New Yorker, The New York Times Book Review,* and *Paris Review.* He has received three Pushcart Prizes, and two selections in *Best American Poetry.* He is currently serving as a judge for the 2021 National Book Award in fiction. An earlier version of "Television, Trees" originally appeared in *Love Song with Motor Vehicles,* BOA Editions, 2003.

**Gail Peck** has published nine books of poetry, including *An Instant Out of TIme; The Braided Light; Within Two Rooms;* and *Counting The Lost.* Her poems and essays have appeared in *The Southern Review, The Greensboro Review, The Louisville Review, Cimarron Review,* and many others. She is the recipient of the 2021 Irene Blair Honeycutt Lifetime Achievement Award. "Transport" is from *Counting the Lost,* Main Street Rag Publishing Company, Charlotte, North Carolina, 2015.

**Diana Pinckney** is the author of five books of poetry. Her work has been published in *Cave Wall, Kakalak, Still Point Arts Quarterly, Streetlight,* and other journals, both print and online. Pinckney has been awarded the 2010 Ekphrasis Prize; *Atlanta Review*'s 2012 International Prize; and the 2018 Prime Number Magazine Award for Poetry. "Fallen Gardens" was first published in *Green Mountains Review,* 20th Anniversary Double Issue.

**David Potorti** is the co-founder of September 11th Families for Peaceful Tomorrows. He served as the literature and theater director for the North Carolina Arts Council and is active in ONE Wake, a non-partisan, multi-ethnic, multi-issue group of religious congregations, associations, and other non-profits in the Wake County, North Carolina area, implementing systemic changes within society to achieve the common good.

**Dannye Romine Powell**'s fifth collection, *In the Sunroom with Raymond Carver* (Press 53), won the 2020 Roanoke-Chowan Award for Poetry. She's a two-time winner of the Randall Jarrell Poetry Award, and she's received fellowships in poetry from the NEA, the North Carolina Arts Council, and Yaddo. Her poems have appeared in *Beloit Poetry Journal, Poetry, Ploughshares* and others. "Loss Calls the Cops" is from *A Necklace of Bees*, The University of Arkansas Press, 2008.

**Gretchen Steele Pratt** is the author of *One Island* (Anhinga Press). Her work has recently appeared in *Southern Review, Beloit Poetry Journal, Gettysburg Review, Poetry Daily* and *Ecotone*. She lives in Matthews, North Carolina, with her husband and three children, and teaches at the University of North Carolina at Charlotte. "Beneath September" was first published in *Pleiades Magazine*.

**Barbara Presnell** has published five poetry books, including *Blue Star* (Press 53) and *Piece Work* (CSU Poetry Center). Poetry and essays appear in *Cumberland River Review, storySouth, Kestrel,* and *The Southern Review*. A recipient of the North Carolina Arts Council Fellowship and the Linda Flowers Prize, she lives in Lexington, North Carolina. "Planting the Garden," was first published in *Pedestal Magazine*.

**David Radavich**'s latest narrative collection, *America Abroad* (2019), is a companion to his earlier *America Bound* (2007). Recent lyric collections are *Middle-East Mezze* (2011) and *The Countries We Live In* (2014). His plays have been performed across the U.S. and in Europe.

**Kaye Nelson Ratliff** earned an MSW from UNC-Chapel Hill in 1986. She practiced clinical social work and consultation until 2015. President of Anson County Writers Club, she has published one book of poetry, *The River Running Through Him*. She resides with her husband in Wadesboro, North Carolina.

**Glenis Redmond** is a nationally renowned, award-winning poet and teaching artist. She co-founded a literary program called Peace Voices in her hometown of Greenville, South Carolina from 2012–2019. Glenis is also a Kennedy Center Teaching Artist and a Cave Canem poet and North Carolina Literary Recipient. In 2020, Glenis became a recipient of South Carolina's highest award, The Governor's Award for the Arts. Her work has been showcased on NPR and PBS and most recently published in *Orion Magazine*, *The North Carolina Literary Review*, *Obsidian Literature and Arts in the African Diaspora*, *StorySouth*, *About Place*, and *Carolina Muse*. Her latest book, *The Listening Skin* will be published by Four Way Books in 2022.

**Adrian Rice,** from Belfast, now living in Hickory, is an established poet on both sides of the Atlantic. *The Mason's Tongue* was short-listed for the Christopher Ewart-Biggs Memorial Literary Prize, and nominated for the Irish Times Prize for Poetry. His poem "Breath" was a Pushcart Prize nominee, and a *Guardian* "Poem of the Week." Rice is a Lecturer at Appalachian State University. His latest book is *The Strange Estate: New & Selected Poems 1986-2017* (Press 53).

**David Rigsbee** is the author of, most recently, *This Much I Can Tell You* and *Not Alone in My Dancing: Essays and Reviews*, both from Black Lawrence Press. His translation of Dante's *Paradiso* is forthcoming from Salmon Poetry.

**Kevin Rippin** lives and writes in Greensboro. North Carolina. His poetry book, *Amber Drive*, was published in 2018 by Main Street Rag Press. Last year (2020), his poems appeared in *Appalachian Edge*, *Pine Mountain Sand & Gravel*, *Poems from the Heron Clan VII*, and *The Lyre*. Rippin was also awarded the second place prize/publication by the Canadian magazine, *Into the Void*, for his story "Zoloft." That story was also nominated for a Pushcart Prize. "American Back Porch" is from *Amber Drive*.

**Pat Riviere-Seel** is the author of four poetry collections, most recently, *When There Were Horses* (Main Street Rag Publishing Company, Fall 2021). Her chapbook, *The Serial Killer's Daughter,* won the Roanoke-Chowan Award. Before earning her MFA from Queens University of Charlotte, she worked as a newspaper journalist, an editor, a publicist, and a lobbyist.

**Phillip Shabazz** is the author of three poetry collections, and a novel in verse. His poetry has been included in the anthologies, *Literary Trails of the North Carolina Piedmont: A Guidebook* and *Home Is Where: African-American Poetry from the Carolinas*. Some previous publication credits in journals include, *Fine Lines*, *Galway*

*Review, Hamilton Stone Review, Hamline Lit, Impossible Task, Mason Street Review, New Critique, On The Seawall,* and *the Original Van Gogh's Ear Anthology.* "For the Moonflower" was first published in the *Galway Review.*

**Alan Shapiro**'s new book of poems, *Proceed to Check Out,* will be published by the University of Chicago Press in the spring of 2021. "Manhood" is from *Against Translation,* University of Chicago Press, 2019.

**Maureen Sherbondy**'s most recent poetry book is *Dancing with Dali* (FutureCycle Press, 2020). Her poems have appeared in *The Oakland Review, Prelude, Litro, European Judaism,* and other journals. She teaches English at Alamance Community College. Maureen lives in Durham, North Carolina.

**Nancy Simpson** authored three poetry collections: *Across Water* and *Night Student* (both published by State Street Press), and most recently *Living Above the Frost Line: New and Selected Poems,* the first in the Laureate Series, published (2010) at Carolina Wren Press.

**Mark Smith-Soto**'s books include *Our Lives Are Rivers* (University Press of Florida, 2003); *Any Second Now* (Main Street Rag Publishing Co., 2006); and *Time Pieces* (Main Street Rag Publishing Co., 2015). *Fever Season: Selected Poetry of Ana Istarú* (2010) and *Berkeley Prelude: A Lyrical Memoir* (2013) were published by Unicorn Press. "Manhattan Buddha" was first published in *The Sun,* Chapel Hill, North Carolina, 2001.

**D. M. Spratley** is a third-generation poet, author of the micro-chapbook *Some Tricks I Was Born Knowing* (Ghost City Press), winner of the Sundress Press 2020 Poetry Broadside Contest, and a North Carolina Arts Council Fellow. She lives in Durham with her partner, Becca, and their dogs, Goosebumps and Cedar.

**Shelby Stephenson** served as Poet Laureate of North Carolina from 2015 to 2018. He was editor of *Pembroke Magazine* for thirty-two years. He is a member of the Society of Distinguished Alumni, Department of English, University of Wisconsin-Madison. The author of many books, his most recent is *Shelby's Lady: The*

*Hog Poems.* "September Mourning" is from *The Hunger of Freedom,* Red Dashboard Press, 2014.

**Dee Stribling** is a poet focusing on culture and landscape. A Poet Laureate of Hillsborough North Carolina, she has authored several poetry chapbooks and is a Sundress Academy for the Arts poetry winner. Her full-length poetry collection will be available from Hermit Feathers Press late 2021.

**Julie Suk** is the prize-winning author of seven volumes of poetry, among them *The Angel of Obsession; The Dark Takes Aim;* and *What I Forgot to Say.* She is the co-editor of *Bear Crossings: An Anthology of North American Poets,* and is included in *The Autumn House Anthology of Contemporary American Poetry.* "Where We Are" was first published by *Shenandoah.*

**Chuck Sullivan** is the author of a number of volumes of poetry, including *Vanishing Species* and *Zen Matchbox.* Of his poem in this anthology, he says: "I read my poem at the Selwyn Pub in Charlotte two eves before Christmas 2001. When I was finished, five couples who didn't know each other, all from New York City, came up to me and shared their stories of loved ones lost. We shared a round or two and tears, as well. I was so blessed to have met them." "A Carol at Ground Zero" is from *Zen Matchbox,* Main Street Rag Publishing, Charlotte, NC, 2008.

**Gilda Morina Syverson** is a poet, writer, artist and educator. She has published two books of poetry: *Facing the Dragon* and *In This Dream Everything Remains Inside.* Gilda's writing has appeared in numerous literary journals, magazines and anthologies. Her award-winning poems and prose include her memoir, *My Father's Daughter, From Rome to Sicily.* "Four Years Later, It's a Deeper Sad" is from *Facing the Dragon.*

**Richard Allen Taylor** of Charlotte, North Carolina, holds an MFA in Creative Writing from Queens University of Charlotte. The author of three poetry collections, most recently *Armed and Luminous* (2016) from Main Street Rag Publishing Company, Taylor co-founded and, for several years, co-edited the journal *Kakalak.*

**Amber Flora Thomas** is the author of the volumes: *Eye of Water,* winner of the 2004 Cave Canem Poetry Prize; *The Rabbits Could Sing;* and *Red Channel in the Rupture.* She is the recipient of the

Dylan Thomas American Poet Prize, the Richard Peterson Prize, and the Ann Stanford Prize. She teaches at East Carolina University.

**Jay Wentworth** is a retired Appalachian State University professor of Interdisciplinary Studies. As a teacher, his goal was to provide young people with contexts for learning and transformation; as a poet, his goal is to share the processes by which he has met the world and been transformed.

**Jacinta V. White** is the founder of The Word Project and *Snapdragon: A Journal of Art & Healing.* Her latest poetry collection, *Resurrecting the Bones,* (Press 53) is inspired by her visits to African American churches and cemeteries. Jacinta is the recipient of numerous awards and recognitions, and has work featured in many publications.

**Laurie Wilcox-Meyer's** third collection, *Conversation in the Key of Blue,* was published by Main Street Rag Publishing, 2020. She lives in the French Broad River basin in the Blue Ridge Mountains of North Carolina where she often spots bears while hiking and meditating about her next poem. Her poetry is also shaped by her upbringing in Louisiana, where she played Chopin and dodged alligators while waterskiing.

**Cheryl Wilder** is the author of *Anything That Happens*, a Tom Lombardo Poetry Selection (Press 53), and the chapbook, *What Binds Us* (Finishing Line Press). A founder and editor of *Waterwheel Review*, Cheryl earned her MFA from Vermont College of Fine Arts. Her home is near the Haw River.

**Dede Wilson's** seven poetry collections include *Glass*, finalist, Persephone Press Award; *Sea of Small Fears*, winner, Main Street Rag Chapbook Competition; *One Nightstand, Eliza: The New Orleans Years*; and *Mrs. H. and Her Tooty-Falooty Ways*, all from Main Street Rag Publishing Company; *Near Waking*, Finishing Line Press; and *Under the Music of Blue*, FutureCycle Press. "Voice of the Wreckage" originally appeared in the chapbook, *Glass*, published in 1998 by Scots Plaid Press. It appeared again in a full-length collection, *Under the Music of Blue.*

**Emily Herring Wilson** is a poet and nonfiction writer with a lifetime commitment to education, economic equality, and children, and who will spend the rest of her life (She is a grandmother) trying to recover America. Poetry sustains her.

**Allan Wolf**'s many picture books, poetry collections, and young adult novels celebrate his love of research, history, science, and poetry. He is a Los Angeles Times Book Prize finalist, two-time winner of the North Carolina Young Adult Book Award, and recipient of New York's Bank Street College Claudia Lewis Award for Poetry.

**Annie Woodford** is the author of *Bootleg* (Groundhog Poetry Press, 2019), a runner-up for the 2020 Weatherford Award for Appalachian Poetry. Her second book won Mercer University's 2020 Adrienne Bond Award and is forthcoming in 2022. She lives in Deep Gap, North Carolina, and teaches at Wilkes Community College.

In 2003, **John Thomas York** was named Outstanding English Teacher of the Year by the North Carolina English Teachers Association. In 2012, Press 53 published his collection, *Cold Spring Rising*. His work has appeared recently in *Appalachian Journal*, *Cold Mountain Review*, and *Tar River Poetry*.

**Taylor A. Young** is a writer, and musician from South Florida, by way of Raleigh, North Carolina. In 2021, Young's prose piece, "Remembrance," received Honorable Mention in the North Carolina Writers' Network's Jacobs/Jones African American Literary Prize Competition. Her work centers the Black experience in America and across the Black diaspora.

**Thom Young** is the happiest person in Kansas City, Missouri, where they moved to from their beloved mountains. They make home in a Jazz Age hotel with two cats: Pretzel and Mr Mr. Their epic poem *BESPOKE* is available from St. Andrews University Press, Laurinburg, North Carolina. "Trope" appears in their second collection, albeit in a drastically different form, *The Private Life of Adonis*.

**Lisa Zerkle**'s poem "Relics of the Great Acceleration" won the North Carolina Writers' Network 2017 Randall Jarrell Poetry Competition. She is the curator of 4X4CLT, a public art and poetry series of the Charlotte Center for Literary Arts, and an MFA candidate at Warren Wilson College. "In Flight" was first published in *The Broad River Review*.

CPSIA information can be obtained
at www.ICGtesting.com
Printed in the USA
BVHW072113220821
614829BV00008B/18/J

9 781950 413386